The Complete Guides to Horses and Ponies

UNDERSTANDING HORSES&PONIES

Jackie Budd

Gareth Stevens Publishing
MILWAUKEE

For a free color catalog describing Gareth Stevens Publishing's list of high-quality books and multimedia programs, call 1-800-542-2595 (USA) or 1-800-461-9120 (Canada). Gareth Stevens Publishing's Fax: (414) 225-0377.

Library of Congress Cataloging-in-Publication Data

Budd, Jackie.
Understanding horses & ponies / by Jackie Budd.
p. cm. — (The complete guides to horses and ponies)
Includes bibliographical references (p. 64) and index.
Summary: Discusses the history, physical characteristics, lifestyles, communication, and education of horses and ponies, as well as their interaction with people.
ISBN 0-8368-2448-2 (lib. bdg.)
1. Horses—Juvenile literature.   2. Ponies—Juvenile literature.   3. Horses—Behavior—Juvenile literature.   4. Ponies—Behavior—Juvenile literature.
[1. Horses. 2. Ponies.] I. Title. II. Series: Budd, Jackie. Complete guides to horses and ponies.
SF302.B84   1999
636.1—dc21   99-20471

First published in North America in 1999 by
Gareth Stevens Publishing
1555 North RiverCenter Drive, Suite 201
Milwaukee, Wisconsin 53212 USA

This U.S. edition © 1999 by Gareth Stevens, Inc. Created with original © 1998 under the title Understanding Ponies by Ringpress Books, Ltd. and Jackie Budd, P. O. Box 8, Lydney, Gloucestershire, United Kingdom, GL15 6YD, in association with Horse & Pony Magazine. All photographs courtesy of Horse & Pony Magazine. Additional end matter © 1999 by Gareth Stevens, Inc.

The publisher would like to thank Jill Groff for her assistance with the accuracy of the text. Ms. Groff has shown hunters and jumpers successfully throughout the United States and South America. Students she has trained have won competitions throughout the United States — including ribbons at prestigious horse shows, such as the National Pony Finals and the National Horse Show.

Printed in Mexico

1 2 3 4 5 6 7 8 9 03 02 01 00 99

Contents

Born to run

It is twilight. The cougar lies in the long grass, motionless, belly pressed to the ground. Its eye is fixed on a small band of horses some distance away. There are young ones that might make easy prey.

The stallion cannot relax. He paces around the edge of the group, eyes scanning the horizon, ears flicking back and forth. Only the eldest mare shares his restlessness. Like him, she knows the time between daylight and darkness is most likely to hide dangers for the herd.

A twig snaps. Instantly, the two horses' heads jerk up as one, ears straining in the direction of the sound, muscles taut, every sense on full alert. In a fraction of a second, the others have picked up on the cues. Foals are nudged to their feet by anxious mothers, youngsters' play stops abruptly, and shared neck nibbles between friends are abandoned.

Below: **A pony's instincts tell him not to take even the slightest risk. A hunted animal rarely gets a second chance.**

Then they are gone in a swirl of dust, tails high, and hooves thudding on the hard, dry ground. The eldest mare leads the getaway. The stallion drives the group on from the rear, checking for vulnerable stragglers.

No need to think twice about which way to go; the horses gallop with barely a glance at the ground beneath their feet. The eldest mare knows every inch for a hundred miles around, blindfolded. One visit is enough for her to memorize every watering place, shelter, patch of sweet grass, strange-smelling plant, bog, and ravine.

At last, the horses begin to slow, taking their lead from the mare. In time, the fear subsides. A calm returns to the herd. One by one, the horses return to picking at the grass. The foals nuzzle their mothers for reassurance. Another day — another escape.

Let's go!

I wonder why...

horses let us ride them and tell them what to do when they are so much bigger and stronger than we are. Horses like an easy, trouble-free life as part of a team. They feel safe when everybody is getting along and someone who has their best interests at heart is in charge, just like in the herd. Now that someone is you!

Above: Getting along with your pony involves trusting each other.

Natural instincts

Do you ever spend time leaning over a fence, just watching ponies in a field? If so, you know that sometimes they can be grazing or dozing quietly, when all of a sudden, off they go, thundering across to the far fence-line, around and back again, tails to the sky, bucking and snorting!

Even though you can put a saddle and bridle on your pony, inside he's every bit as wild as the horses on the plains.

Getting along together

We all love horses and ponies because they are real, live animals with minds of their own, yet they do not mind going along with our ideas about being ridden, jumping ditches, and following trails. Sometimes, our friendship has problems because we don't think like horses, and horses don't think like humans. If we cannot get on the same wavelength, there's bound to be a communication problem.

It is easy to believe that animals are not as smart as humans, without really stopping to consider why they think and act as they do. How much better riders and pony lovers we would be if, instead of trying to just boss them around, we took the time to find out what is going on inside their heads.

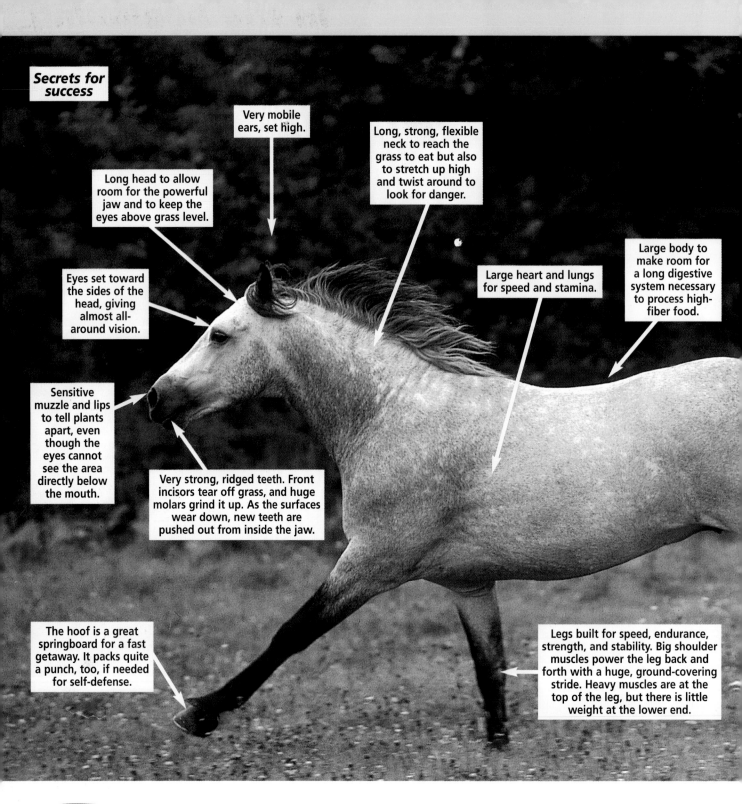

Secrets for success

Very mobile ears, set high.

Long, strong, flexible neck to reach the grass to eat but also to stretch up high and twist around to look for danger.

Long head to allow room for the powerful jaw and to keep the eyes above grass level.

Large heart and lungs for speed and stamina.

Large body to make room for a long digestive system necessary to process high-fiber food.

Eyes set toward the sides of the head, giving almost all-around vision.

Sensitive muzzle and lips to tell plants apart, even though the eyes cannot see the area directly below the mouth.

Very strong, ridged teeth. Front incisors tear off grass, and huge molars grind it up. As the surfaces wear down, new teeth are pushed out from inside the jaw.

The hoof is a great springboard for a fast getaway. It packs quite a punch, too, if needed for self-defense.

Legs built for speed, endurance, strength, and stability. Big shoulder muscles power the leg back and forth with a huge, ground-covering stride. Heavy muscles are at the top of the leg, but there is little weight at the lower end.

Super surv

Horses are among the animal kingdom's champion survivors. The pony you ride could trace his family tree back fifty million years! How did horses manage to get so good at the survival game?

Overcoming obstacles

The horse is one of nature's most adaptable creatures. Every time an obstacle is thrown in his path to threaten his existence, he finds a way of overcoming it.

In the Miocene period (5-23 million years ago), the climate slowly became cooler and drier. The lush swamps turned to arid, open grasslands. The ancestors of your pony survived these changes by gradually trading their padded, three-toed feet for single hooves that could gallop. Their senses fine-tuned to detect predators just seconds before they had a chance to pounce.

"Equus" was the most successful of all the prehistoric types of horses, and he soon traveled all over the globe.

Very sensitive skin with twitch muscles to remove flies. Hair grows thicker or thinner depending on the weather conditions. Plenty of mane and tail hair for extra warmth and fly-whisking.

The legs are long so the grass does not get in the way of either movement or sight.

ivors

Meeting up with humans

Early humans hunted a few weak stragglers from passing horse herds. They used the meat for food, the bones for tools, and the hide for clothing.

Later, when humans settled and became farmers, they realized how useful horses could be in other ways. Drawings, carvings, and sculptures from ancient civilizations show that, by about 2000 B.C., horses were ridden by humans. They were also harnessed to chariots.

Horses provided transportation to places far away and at speeds never dreamed of before. Now humans could visit and explore other lands. They could build empires. They could trade goods and services with other peoples. They could fight wars.

Horses were key to the progress of civilization. Thanks to the many jobs they could do and their amazing willingness to do them, horses became prized and valued and were even worshiped.

Once again, it was fortunate that the horse was so adaptable. Since the last Ice Age (around eighteen thousand years ago), vegetation spread so quickly across Europe that the wild horses of the plains confronted another obstacle to their survival — thick forests. They faced extinction at last.

The new partnership with humans meant the horse was going to make another narrow escape. Only this time, to survive, he had to give up his freedom.

Left: The horse was the last animal to be domesticated, many thousands of years after goats, sheep, cattle, pigs, and dogs began to share their lives with humans. The donkey *(pictured)* is actually a descendant of a separate equine species, the African wild ass.

Below: A long, strong, and flexible neck has its advantages.

Prehistory to today's ponies

Nature came up with a basic design for horses that seemed to work well. It then polished this even more by giving horses characteristics to suit the climate and surroundings of the particular region where they lived. This is how different breeds and types of horses and ponies began.

All horses originated from primitive herds that migrated to Asia from America before the melting icecaps cut off the land bridges. For some mysterious reason, equines then died out in their home continent and were only reintroduced by the Spanish Conquistadores in the fifteenth century. Some horses settled in hot, dry regions. Others traveled farther west and north to colder, damper places.

Mix and match

Over the centuries, since the time when horses were first domesticated, people have tried to create new types of horses for specific purposes through crossbreeding.

Very few purebreds remain in the world. Of the more than two hundred breeds in existence today, most have been created by crossbreeding. Some, however, have had less interference than others. The Exmoor pony, for example, probably looks very much like it did a thousand years ago. Most of today's breeds have carefully kept registers, or Stud Books, with recorded details about the individuals.

Thanks to stables, blankets, and premium feeds, even horses that evolved to live in hot climates can be kept and bred in colder countries. The result is a wonderful kaleidoscope of horses and ponies living around the world today.

What happened to the wild horses?

Some groups of horses still live free — the mustangs of America, the brumbies of Australia, and the white horses of the Camargue in southern France. They are feral horses, meaning that their ancestors were domesticated horses that escaped or that they have been interfered with in some way by humans. Probably the nearest we have to a real wild horse is Przewalski's horse from the Mongolian steppes. This ancient horse looks as though it could have galloped right out of a prehistoric cave painting.

Above: The Arab is typical of the hot-blood type, which adapted to life in the searing heat and dust of the desert. Its thin skin and short, fine hair help the blood lose heat easily. Flared nostrils and a high tail carriage are also part of the cooling system. Long, fine legs with small, hard hooves are built for speed and allow plenty of air movement around and underneath the oval-shaped body.

Above: Compare the Arab to these Shires, examples of a cold-blood type. These equine heavyweights evolved in cool marshy or woodland regions. Their priority is to keep body warmth in, not let it out. Thick skins, hairy coats, bushy manes and tails, slit-like nostrils, stubby legs, and round, chunky bodies all help keep in the warmth. A long head warms the air before it reaches the lungs. Big, flat feet are well suited to wet ground.

I wonder why...

they are called hot-bloods and cold-bloods. It has nothing to do with the body temperature, which is about 100.4° Fahrenheit (38°Celsius) for all horses. These terms refer to the sensitive, quick-reacting nature of the hot-blood horses compared to the generally slower-moving and slower-thinking cold-bloods.

Above: Warm-bloods are produced by crossing hot- and cold-blood types to get the best of both. The goal is to create a horse with the classy look and athletic ability of the hot-bloods and the strength and toughness of the cold-bloods. Many modern sports horses are warm-bloods.

Above: Pony breeds evolved from smaller hot- or cold-blood horses that found themselves in areas where conditions were very harsh — such as high, mountainous places isolated from contact with other horses or humans. These native ponies may not have grown very big, but what they lacked in size they made up for in sense.

Below: Przewalski's horse is believed to be a separate species from the horses known today. It almost died out but has recently been bred in zoos.

Above: The Thoroughbred is a completely artificial breed, created in Europe in the seventeenth and eighteenth centuries from Arab and other eastern horses. It was bred purely for its speed.

Pick a pony

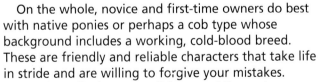

Are all chestnuts fiery redheads?

Every type of horse or pony has his very own type of personality. When it comes to purchasing a horse or pony, it is best to educate yourself on their various characteristics. Just as evolution adapted some horses' bodies to survival in the desert and others to a snow-swept mountainside, it also adapted their personalities.

Horses and ponies all tend to be nervous creatures. They are tuned to sense danger. Hot-blood breeds, however, are the flightiest of all. As a general rule, they are quick moving, quick thinking, and highly strung. This is because they evolved on open plains shared with speedy and cunning predators.

Ponies with a lot of Thoroughbred and Arab blood tend to behave this way, too. It takes an experienced owner to keep their trust and to ride and handle them sensitively. They can be very intelligent and very talented athletes, but they are often easily upset if things don't go quite right. They need requests to be explained to them very carefully and consistently in order to feel confident. Being from warmer climates, this type of pony also feels the cold easily. He will need extra care, particularly in winter, when he will have to be brought into a stable at night with a cozy blanket and premium feed.

Left: **Within every breed is the wise, old character that has seen and done it all. These "schoolmaster" ponies are perfect for a first-time owner.**

On the whole, novice and first-time owners do best with native ponies or perhaps a cob type whose background includes a working, cold-blood breed. These are friendly and reliable characters that take life in stride and are willing to forgive your mistakes.

They have lively personalities, too. Life up there on the challenging moors and mountains required plenty of "native cunning."

These ponies are good at thinking for themselves — which can come in very handy when you forget to ask for that extra stride between the jumps. Chances are your pony will put it in anyway.

In addition to all their other fine qualities, native and cob types are tough and hardy. They are able to winter out quite happily with good, basic daily care. They are less prone to getting themselves into trouble or having health problems than the flightier and finer types of ponies.

Right: Novice riders usually do best with chunky pony or cob types that are easy to care for and ride. Leave the challenge of a pony with hot blood in him to experienced riders.

Above: Przewalski's horse and the Exmoor *(pictured)* have coloring typical of the most primitive breeds.

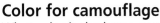

Above: Duns often have an eel-stripe down their backs and even a few faint stripes on their legs, similar to zebras.

Color for camouflage

What color is the horse or pony you ride? Does his coloring provide you with any clues about who his age-old ancestors could have been?

The very earliest horses were probably mottled in color to blend in with the scattered light filtering through the tropical rain forest. Dapples on grays and even some of the bays and chestnuts could be the remains of this prehistoric camouflage. In just the same way, "eel" stripes down the spine and the faint "zebra" stripes on the backs of the legs

Left: A dappled coat once helped this horse's ancestors hide in the forest vegetation.

of breeds like the Highland pony hint at the close relationship between ponies and their striped cousins from the African savanna. Cave paintings show most primitive horses as dun or light brown with pale bellies and darker manes and tails. This color blended in with both the frozen tundra of the far north and the dry Asian and African plains. It is still common in the very oldest native breeds, such as the Shetland, Highland, Icelandic, and Norwegian Fjord.

Even the most modern and refined breeds, such as the Thoroughbred, can still show this pale muzzle and flanks in a bay-colored horse.

Horses and ponies can be bred for color just like the various other features. One color that is difficult to reproduce is palomino. Even two palominos mated together do not always result in a palomino foal.

Colorful characters

There is no scientific evidence that color affects character. Coat colors, such as chestnut and gray, can indicate sensitive skin, however. If you are looking for a pony to buy, it is best not to set your heart on a particular color or you may miss out on the very pony that is perfect for you in every other way except his hair color.

A pony's world

Above: **A great deal of pony behavior is actually based on reflex action designed to keep him alive.**

Many animals can sense, see, feel, or hear things that humans cannot. Dogs inhabit a world colored with a rainbow of smells. Bats fly using radar. Birds migrate using Earth's magnetic field as a map. Every animal, including the horse, has evolved senses finely tuned for survival in its own particular environment.

Even though your pony doesn't have to worry about a lion creeping up on him, he still operates under exactly the same super-sensitive early warning system as the ponies of centuries ago.

Rapid reflexes

A reflex is an automatic response by the body that takes place instantly without the brain thinking about it. Many survival reactions are reflexes, genetically programmed into an animal's brain and nervous system to help the

animal react quickly in a crisis. If we could step inside a pony's head and look out at the world through his eyes, we would see that many of his actions that may seem unusual to us are, in fact, almost like reflexes to him. His responses are designed to keep him alive. Amazingly, humans can train a horse or pony to overcome many natural fears. It is not surprising, however, that the horse or pony finds it hard to blot out certain terrors completely. He may never understand that plastic bags blowing around and tractors passing by are harmless to him. Fears of innocent objects like these are all part of a horse's instinct to survive.

Another world

When we begin to look at the way other animals experience their world, we realize just how limited human senses really are. It is as though humans see the world through peepholes. We may go through an entire day without really hearing or seeing many of the things in our environment. We pick up only a fraction of what really happens around us.

The world as a pony sees it is sometimes the same as a human's, but not always. Horses have senses and ways of thinking that are sometimes better than, sometimes not as good as, and sometimes simply different from humans. Often this is the reason for misunderstandings between ponies and people.

Even when similarities exist between ponies and people, your pony will interpret what he senses according to a pony's needs, not a human's.

If your pony escaped to join a herd of wild horses, he probably could manage quite well. His survival skills might be a bit rusty compared to his companions. Despite thousands of years of domestication, however, horses and ponies are still quite able to look out for themselves if they have to.

Above: Have you ever stopped to think about how skilled ponies are at balance and coordination? They have to organize four legs and a large body to stay upright at all speeds over all terrain. Then they are asked to carry the weight of a rider and jump obstacles, too!

Below: Within minutes of being born, a foal can coordinate his movements well enough to be on his feet and running with the herd.

body sense

One sensation members of the animal kingdom share is an awareness of our own bodies. None of us would survive very long if we had to constantly think about exactly where our legs and feet are to keep ourselves from falling over.

Watch a group of ponies playing in a field — bucking and cavorting, spinning, and racing off. Horses are great at controlling and coordinating their movements without thinking about it. Reflexes are continually telling the horse or pony which muscles to use to help him stay in balance on his feet throughout any change of speed or direction. Your pony is very good at judging how tall and wide he is, too, but doesn't always take into account the extra height and width of a rider. Please be kind and understanding about this.

What a pony sees

Sight is one of the horse's most important abilities. It is also the sense where there is the biggest difference between a pony's perspective and your own.

A prey animal must have a good view all around itself to be on the look-out for the enemy. Horses' eyes are huge for animals of their size. These big eyes are set on the sides of their head because they need to be able to see not only in front, but also to each side. By rolling the eyes back, they can even watch for enemies while they are eating.

Compare your pony's eyes to your own or to a dog's or cat's. Unlike horses, hunting animals do not need to worry about an attack from behind. What predators need is two eyes on the front of their head so they can focus very precisely and judge the distance of an object in order to successfully attack. To a horse, calculating depth like this is not important. Getting a few strides ahead of a predator is!

Below: To a pony, any movement from the rear could be a threat. Older, more experienced horses do get used to things happening behind them, but you should still take care and give him fair warning that you are there.

Above: A dog's eyes let him focus very precisely. With eyes set to the side, a horse is not as good at judging depth and distance but has a much wider field of vision and is very sensitive to movement.

Horses can see 340 of the 360 degrees around them, whether they are grazing, galloping, or simply standing still. They have only two narrow blind spots, under the muzzle and directly behind them.

Wide-angle vision

The horse's field of vision is enormous. The draw-back is that, although he is designed to notice the slightest movement, the horse is not very good at registering details of distance, depth, and dimension. This is because most of the area down each side of the horse is covered only by the sight of one eye. A pony sees the world as if through two completely separate, wide-angle cameras, one on each side of his head.

Down each side, the images are flat and fuzzy. He can get sharp, three-dimensional shapes only in the narrow area in front of him that both eyes see.

I wonder why . . .

ponies have slits for pupils, instead of circles like our own. This shape enables them to scan the full horizon clearly, no matter how bright the light. The dark, floating blobs on the eyeball filter glaring sunshine.

No wonder your pony sometimes seems to fall over objects literally right under his feet, yet is able to pick out the tiniest of movements on the far horizon!

Getting in focus

We humans have lenses in our eyes that constantly adjust so we can focus on objects at various distances. This is not so automatic for horses and ponies, however. To lock in on objects at different distances, horses and ponies have to raise or lower their heads so light falls onto the best part of each eye's lens. Objects on the far horizon are best seen when the horse or pony raises his head up high. Objects close to the horse or pony require him to bring his head down and his nose in.

Watch your horse or pony as he moves his head, and you will learn to tell what he is looking at and where the particular object is. You can then discover what may be worrying him.

Can horses see colors?

Scientists believe horses and ponies are better at seeing some colors than others. They are best at seeing reds and blues and not quite as good at seeing yellows and greens. To a horse, yellows and greens probably look gray. From a horse's point of view, the spookiest color of all is a glaring, highly reflective one like bright white. You may have guessed this from noticing how upset your horse gets if he sees something like a white plastic bag blow across in front of him.

Seeing in the dark

Wild horses need to be active and alert all night long, so it is fortunate that horses see well in the dark. Horses and ponies find a sudden change from dark to light, or light to dark, startling. The next time you switch on the stable light at night or expect your pony to walk straight from the sunlight into a gloomy trailer, give his eyes time to adjust.

Above: If you place a snack right under your pony's muzzle, he won't be able to see it. His nose gets in the way! Give him time to dip his nose or turn his head slightly to take a look. Keep your hand still and fingers out of the way. He will aim for the place he last saw the food.

Above: Most ponies don't like it when you approach them straight on because you disappear from sight at the last second. If you are trying to catch a pony, approach at an angle to the shoulder so he can see you coming. Give a pat or a stroke on the neck; don't startle a pony by raising your hand sharply in front of his face.

Below: Horses are not as quick to focus their eyes as humans. A pony has to move his head to judge height and distance. So don't hold the head down too tightly!

Left: If a pony wants to have a good look at something, he needs to drop or turn his head and maybe even move his body around. When a pony shies, this is what he is doing. Let him look, rather than just roughly pulling him away.

How a pony hears

Below: This pony's ears are pricked in concentration — intent on a source of interest or a possible threat.

A pony's ears are like radar, constantly swiveling around in the direction of interesting sounds. Set high up on the head, they play an important role in pony-to-pony communication but also work with the eyes as a vital part of the early warning system.

Your pony's ears can move around an amazing 180°, ready to pick up sound from any direction and pinpoint the source with amazing accuracy. The horse can locate the tiniest of noises and even blot out background noise to concentrate on one sound by focusing both ears on it.

With sixteen muscles apiece, each ear can move completely independently. So your pony is easily able to keep one ear on what's coming up ahead and the other on anything going on behind — such as what his rider is up to!

Safe sounds and scary sounds

Many sounds, such as the rattle of a feed bucket, are enjoyable to a horse or pony. There are probably many times, however, when your pony seems to be worried about nothing at all. In fact, he may be hearing a sound that your ears simply cannot pick up.

Strange noises tend to make horses anxious. Horses are always wary of objects and experiences that they do not know for certain are safe. Even the hollow sound of his own feet on a trailer ramp can be very worrying to a youngster that has not traveled before.

Sudden loud bangs or constant clattering is enough to set anyone's nerves on edge, so imagine what it feels like to the super-sensitive ears of your ever-alert pony. Loud, constant music is very bothersome to a horse or pony. Soft, calm music is best for him, rather than blaring, intense rock music.

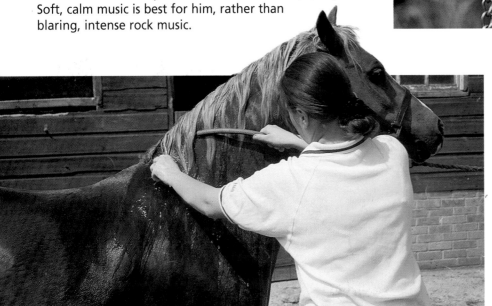

Below: This pony's ears are pricked in concentration — intent on a source of interest or a possible threat.

I wonder why . . .

windy days always seem to unsettle the ponies in the field. Windy, blustery weather masks possible danger signals. On a calm day, when sound carries well, horses feel more content and secure.

Left: Horses tend to be very suspicious of rustling, slithery objects. Who says that a garden hose isn't a snake ready to bite?

Voice-over

We can capitalize on a horse's sensitive hearing by using our voices in many ways. Your pony certainly recognizes your voice, just as he can easily identify his many equine friends by their neighs and whinnies. Speak to him often to warn of your approach, to calm him, to praise or encourage him, to reprimand him if he needs it, and to simply make friends.

Whenever you talk to your horse or pony, the way in which you say something to him is much more important than what you say. Soft, low tones are soothing and reassuring. Sharp, urgent inflections will rile him up. Please remember this when near horses.

Whether you are speaking directly to a pony or not, shouting, loud conversation, and impatient tones will worry him and make him tense.

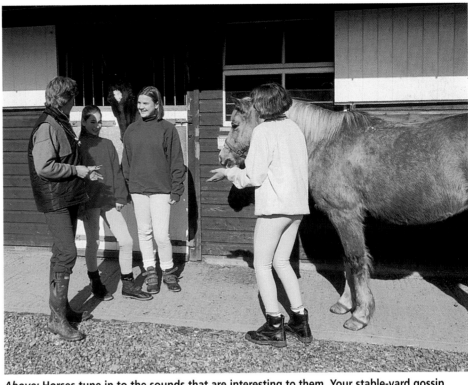

Above: Horses tune in to the sounds that are interesting to them. Your stable-yard gossip is a real bore!

Above: Horse ears can relax to blot out unwanted sounds. They can also press back, tucked away from danger.

Left: Two ears are better than one, especially if they can swivel in different directions!

How a pony uses smell and taste

Horses, like many other animals, actually use smells as a kind of language to talk to each other. Horses' huge nostrils and elongated noses contain deep cavities packed full of nerve endings that detect and interpret smells. If a particularly strange or interesting smell comes along, horses even have a special organ for analyzing it. This is called the Jacobsen's organ. That peculiar "laughing" expression you have seen your horse or pony use is called "flehmen." During flehmen, his top lip pushes the aroma back into the ultra-sensitive organ for analysis.

Above: Stallions use the flehmen action to detect whether a mare is ready to mate. All ponies use this expression at times, usually when they come across a strong or puzzling odor, or even in an unfamiliar situation where they are trying to discover what is going on.

ID cards

Smells tell ponies a great deal about each other. Smells help ponies recognize who is who, even in the dark. Each horse has his own personal scent and also shares a group scent with the herd, which helps keep the group together. During a roll on the ground, a horse grinds the herd's scent into his coat so he feels like he belongs. When a foal is born, his mother will lick him all over to get to know his smell and taste, so she can instantly recognize her own offspring. In this way, she also gives him her scent, too.

Above: Horses are very particular about who their friends are. First encounters are always touch-and-go, until each pony is satisfied that the other smells okay. Watch two ponies meeting for the first time. They approach cautiously and sniff from a safe distance. One whiff is plenty to tell whether the newcomer is a stallion, mare, or gelding. There is plenty of deep snorting, as each takes in a deep breath of the other's scent. This is then memorized.

Above: The lips, whiskers, tongue, and the senses of smell and taste help horses select the tastiest food and leave the rest behind.

If you need to give your pony medicine in his feed, disguise the smell and taste by adding molasses.

Wash your buckets out every time they are used. Nothing stops a pony from eating or drinking quicker than the smell of stale food or water.

Above: Rolling grinds the herd's scent into the coat.

Scent signals

A wild horse gets all kinds of information about his surroundings using his sense of smell — where there is water, the possibility of a lurking predator, or the knowledge that he is safe within his own herd's territory.

Some smells convey danger. A pony's abilities to smell and to taste work together to make sure he eats only the best grasses and passes over any plants that may be harmful.

Most ponies like sweet-tasting things but are wary of anything with a bitter taste. Bitterness is a feature of most poisonous plants. You may have noticed how incredibly smart horses are at sorting and sifting with their lips and tongue. Not only can they pick out the tasty grasses from the less tasty ones, but they can easily identify every worming granule or other type of medicine that is hidden in their feed. Even if they do take a mouthful and then have second thoughts, they can manage to sort it out and spit out the unwanted ingredients.

Wonderful whiskers

Because ponies cannot see the ends of their noses, their super-sensitive whiskers are crucial for telling them how far their nose is from the ground, recognizing plants, and carefully sniffing and touching other horses. A pony uses his whiskers like antennae to help him "see." It is very unfair, even cruel, to cut whiskers off just because you think he looks more elegant without them.

it's a fact!

Horses can even smell fear. Fear is conveyed by subtle scents called pheromones produced by all animals (including humans) when they are alerted or aroused. Quick to read any "danger" message, horses will instantly be at the ready for "fight-or-flight" whenever they detect these. So try to be brave next time you approach that big ditch cross-country!

Left: By licking the foal all over after it is born, the mare gives him an identity tag that links him to her and the herd. Even in darkness, horses recognize each other by scent.

it's a fact!

A stallion picks up the scent of a mare in season from a distance of 650 feet (200 meters)!

I wonder why . . .

my pony always goes to the bathroom the minute he gets into his clean stable. To a pony, things have to smell right. There is nothing like a pony's own odor to provide a feeling of security and familiarity.

Above: Ponies avoid objects with bad smells. For this reason, some can be very picky about what they eat. It is almost impossible to hide medicine in their feed.

Left: Give a pony some time to sniff you when you first meet. It's his way of getting to know you.

Above: Touch plays a big part in a horse's life.

Touching and feeling

Just like our own, a pony's skin is full of cells sensitive to different kinds of feelings and pressures. Some areas of the body are particularly sensitive to touch, such as the whiskers, the neck, the withers, and under the belly. The gums, where the bit lies, feel pain easily — the best reason of all to be light and easy with our hands.

Do not irritate a pony by touching him carelessly. Some breeds, such as Arabs and Thoroughbreds, have very thin, sensitive skin and need to be groomed very gently. Individual ponies of any breed can be especially sensitive.

On the whole, horses prefer to be touched considerately, but not nervously. Sometimes lightly dabbing at a ticklish pony will annoy him just as much as scrubbing too hard with a stiff brush. You will soon know if it does by the way he grimaces, swishes his tail, or angrily stamps a foot.

Touch adds an extra dimension to a pony's world. Watch how often horses use it to communicate among themselves. Ponies in a group are constantly touching noses or cementing friendships

it's a fact!

Do you think a pony's feet are hard and unfeeling? A pony is amazingly sensitive to vibrations through the soles of his feet. After all, his survival once depended on staying upright, whatever the ground beneath his hooves. There is a belief that some horses can even tell when an earthquake is coming.

with some mutual neck nibbling. They use touch in courtship and mating. Being able to touch and see other horses can make all the difference between happiness or anxiety when a horse is stabled.

Grooming is just one way of bonding with your pony. When you meet and greet a pony or want to reward him, rub his crest.

Sixth sense?

Some people even think horses are telepathic but because we still have so much to find out about the way their senses work, it is impossible to be sure. Finding the way home from a strange place miles away, sensing the approach of stormy weather, or seeming to know the vet has arrived before he has even come into the stable are the kinds of behaviors that make us wonder about equine Extra Sensory Perception (ESP). Our own senses and abilities to pick up tension and read body language are so limited compared to a horse's, however, that it is very hard to judge what horses can and cannot detect.

close relations

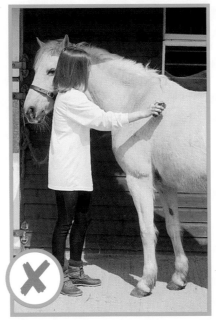
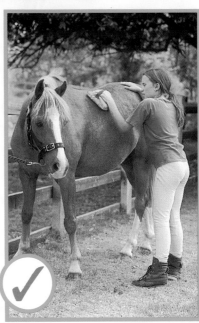

Above: Try not to be nervous around ponies because they pick up your worries and start to become anxious themselves. Brush with bold and confident, but gentle, strokes *(right)* rather than dabbing away at arm's length *(left)*.

Above: Go easy with that sponge or bristly brush! Some body areas are especially sensitive, so it's not surprising many horses and ponies get annoyed by rough grooming or bathing.

Right: Long legs and hooves come in very handy sometimes.

Pony priorities

Above: Avoiding danger usually means running. Fighting back is almost always a second choice, used when escape is not possible.

What things in life are most important to you? When it comes down to what really matters most, the list would probably include having a home to live in, food to eat, and good health. After that, we might put feeling happy and secure with our family and friends, having fun, and perhaps learning new and exciting skills.

Ponies have priorities in life, too. Some of the things on their wish list are much like ours, but others are very different or in a totally different order than yours and mine.

What matters to ponies — even the domesticated ones in the field — is survival. The urge to survive drives all of their behaviors. This urge is what makes a pony act like a pony. Incredibly strong survival priorities influence a pony's every thought — so it is a good idea for a pony owner to understand how much survival means to him.

Survival instincts have been so successful for the horse that they have stayed the same for over fifty million years. A few thousand years of being around humans have made no difference at all to what makes horses and ponies "tick."

1 food and water As all owners know, food is a major preoccupation for ponies. This is fair enough because food is absolutely necessary to survival. Even more crucial is a supply of clean water. Their food and water supply worries horses more than anything else — yet it is the area where there has been the most change between their natural life and the life people have chosen for them.

Above: The uppermost thing on a pony's mind is usually food and water!

2 staying alive Although you may think your pony is safe enough, his instincts are all geared to the constant threat of danger and whether he can escape if the worst situation happens. Because of this drive to protect themselves, horses and ponies are always going

Above: We tend to ignore our horses' urge to reproduce, unless we want to breed a foal.

to be nervous creatures that find it hard to relax, no matter how well trained. The job of humans is to make sure they feel as few threats as possible in their lives.

3 breeding In the wild, horse life revolves around reproduction. With domesticated horses, however, reproduction is handled under very controlled conditions. This is one of the biggest changes humans have made to a horse's natural existence.

4 friends and family Humans enjoy company, but most of us manage quite well by ourselves if need be. A lonely horse, however, is totally miserable because he is programmed to be part of a herd. Without the comfort, security, and friendship of other horses around him, he finds it hard to relax. We can take him out for a ride or even charge around a huge cross-country course, but he needs the companionship of other horses.

It is worth remembering that horses and ponies do not analyze their feelings in the same way humans do. They don't need to be constantly given new things to do or to think about to have a feeling of contentment.

As long as their top priorities are met, they are treated considerately, and they have companions, life is just fine.

Above: Horses can get used to living on their own, but social contact is one of their strongest built-in urges. Think of all the fun this pony is missing out on. Don't make your pony live by himself — find him a friend!

Above: Bonding is a very strong equine instinct, which is one reason why horses have taken so well to domestication. Happiness is having a friend.

Horseplay

A happy pony is a pony that has freedom, water, food, and companionship. When they have some spare time, ponies also enjoy playing, especially when they are youngsters. Horse and pony games — bucking, kicking, racing around, and "spooking" — are usually really about learning survival skills.

From a pony's point of view, there is very little sense at all in wasting energy running around in circles or jumping fences. Even so, that is not to say horses do not like learning new skills and enjoying the activities humans do with them. Horses that are used to activities with humans will feel unhappy about being stuck in a field and never ridden.

ZZZZZZ...

Above: Adult horses sleep two to five hours a day in short stretches. A "stay apparatus" on the elbows and stifles allows them to doze standing up in case a quick getaway is required. Deep sleep, for a few minutes at a time, requires that they sit or lie down.

Lifestyles

Since being domesticated, horses have not only had to get used to living with another species, they have also had to undertake a totally different lifestyle.

Sadly, over the centuries, we have used horses for work, war, and play with little notice of what a horse's real needs are. We have changed his life to suit ourselves. Many traditions are still practiced that show little consideration for a horse's feelings or what he needs to stay fit and well.

No wonder many horses and ponies are unhappy and often show their unhappiness in difficult behavior and health problems. However, there are many ways to make their lives with us closer to what nature intended.

Below: A pony would never choose to be alone.

Two's company

nature In the wild, a horse would never choose to be alone. Being by himself is a very stressful experience. He lives with his family and friends that provide company and security. All day long, he keeps himself busy, eating and interacting with the others. He can pick which ones he wants as friends and avoid the rest.

today Most domesticated horses and ponies spend a lot of time by themselves, either separated into stalls, out riding, or out in the field. Some even live completely alone and have to rely on their owner's brief visits for their only contact with another living being.

Pony-friendly tips
♦ Be sensitive to a pony's likes and dislikes. Avoid stabling sworn enemies next to each other. Let friends be together — but not so much that they become inseparable.

♦ Arrange stabling so that horses can still see and hear others.

♦ Put grills or "talk holes" between stalls so each horse can see and sniff another one.

♦ Find a live-in friend for your pony. The situation is ideal if this is another pony or donkey. Even a sheep, goat, or cow for company is better than being alone.

♦ Spend as much time as possible with your pony to become his special friend.

Below: A stable should be as big, light, and airy as possible. Grills or "talk holes" between stalls reduce boredom, giving horses a chance to "chat" with each other.

it's a fact!

Wild horses or ponies cover a distance of several dozen miles (kilometers) every day, despite having low-quality food and often being burdened with internal worms. How far does your pony go?

I want to be free!

nature Horses evolved as free-roaming creatures, born to run. A wild horse has limitless space in which to move and opportunity to do whatever comes naturally — to go where he wants when he wants, to graze, play, be with his friends, and move away from things he doesn't like or feels threatened by. He takes shelter under a tree or rock face. Horses are naturally claustrophobic — they always avoid any dark, confined space with no way out.

today We expect our horses to live in small, enclosed boxes in which there is barely enough room to turn around. Even though it gives them shelter, a stable must seem like a prison to a pony. Fully stabled horses often spend twenty-three out of every twenty-four hours cooped up. To add to the stress, the horse feels vulnerable because he cannot choose escape even if he wants to. Standing still for so long, with only short bursts of activity, makes him prone to stiffness and injury.

Pony-friendly tips

♦ Turn your pony loose to relax and get some natural exercise for at least a few hours every day, preferably in a field with other ponies.

♦ If there is no alternative to fully stabling your pony, exercise him at least 1-1/2 hours every day in any weather.

♦ Provide as big a stable as possible, with a minimum size of 10 x 10 feet (3 x 3 m).

♦ A cattle yard or pen provides stabled ponies a chance to do some leg stretching.

♦ Make sure your stable is airy and light. Ponies love to be able to see and touch others and to have more than one view — a second half-door or window is ideal.

♦ Beat boredom! Visit your horse or pony often.

Above: If turn-out is limited, a covered shed or pen makes a good compromise in winter, especially for youngsters.

Above: Lack of exercise (combined with overfeeding or unsuitable feeding) is the most common cause of behavioral problems. Exercise is far more important than sweeping up the yard or tidying the tack room. Don't ever let anyone persuade you that it is okay to skip daily exercise for your horse.

Food, *glorious* food!

nature Horses are built to eat grass and plenty of it. In nature, a horse would never eat any kind of grain. He would spend sixteen hours a day feeding. His stomach is not very large, and his digestive system is designed to have small amounts of fibrous food trickling through it continually. In the wild, a horse needs to eat continually because grasses are low in nutrients and energy, and it takes a great amount of them to fuel such a big, strong animal.

today We give our horses two or three square meals a day. Meals are based on grain, jam-packed full of energy and vitamins. Once the bucket is empty, the stabled pony is usually given one net or rack of hay to nibble on. This takes about two hours to finish. There might be twelve hours of waiting before the next mouthful arrives.

Right: Most horses and ponies get more than enough energy and nutrients. Instead of filling the day finding food and eating, food comes in a bucket and only takes a few minutes to eat!

pony-friendly *tips*

Above: Turn your pony out as much as you can. He will amuse himself by searching for grasses to eat.

♦ Turn your pony out often — grasses are his natural food.

♦ Avoid lush pastures. Horses are designed to eat lots of low-grade food. Rich grass can cause serious health problems.

♦ Whenever a pony is stabled, provide lots of hay to eat for fiber. The only time hay intake needs to be controlled is when a pony is on a diet or is doing very hard work.

♦ If your horse eats his hay too quickly, use a small-mesh net to slow him down.

♦ Go easy on the concentrate feed. Most ponies could live quite happily and healthily on grass and/or good-quality hay alone. Concentrate feed is pure energy in a bucket. Give him concentrate feed in winter only (unless your pony is doing lots of shows or long rides), and stick to non-heating nuts and mixes.

♦ It is best to keep feeding routines as close as possible to what nature intended. Feed small portions, but often. Split the daily concentrate total into as many small meals as possible. Feed the concentrate portions at regular intervals.

♦ Use chaff and succulents, such as carrots and apples, with concentrate feed to add fiber and to keep your pony from gulping the meal down too quickly.

♦ Always have clean water available. A thirsty pony will soon become anxious.

♦ Stick to regular feeding times.

♦ Make any changes in your pony's meals or feeding routine gradually to give his delicately balanced digestive system time to adjust. Sudden changes can cause colic.

♦ Give your pony peace and quiet at feeding time. Make sure he is not harassed by other, more dominant, ponies.

♦ If your pony will not keep weight on, check all possible causes — worms, sharp teeth, or incorrect feeding. Think about his environment, too — a thin pony is often a stressed pony.

Stressful stables

Being penned up much of each day is not an ideal way to live. Unfortunately, some stabled horses are literally driven crazy from the boredom and stress of the unnatural way in which they are kept. As a way of coping with their anxieties, sensitive characters develop odd, obsessive behavior, just like the caged animals that pace back and forth behind bars at the zoo. These actions are known as stable vices. This is hardly a fair description because stable vices are not nasty habits that the horse or pony has picked up on purpose. They are behaviors a horse or pony has developed in order to cope.

Almost every stable has its crib-biters, blanket-rippers, and stall-walkers. Some stalls are fitted with anti-weaving grills to keep their occupants from constantly rocking from side-to-side. These acquired habits are unknown among the wild horses.

Although many of these behaviors can be stopped by using various devices, this only treats the symptoms of the horse's unhappiness, not the causes.

Watch a pony with a stable vice carefully to see if anything in particular sets him off or if you can make changes to help him be less stressed. Sadly, most horses become "addicted" to their habit, making it hard to break.

Above: Crib-biting *(top)* and weaving *(bottom)* are ways that sensitive horses cope with a stressful lifestyle.

boredom-busting tips

◆ It is best to turn your horse or pony out into the field as much as possible, preferably with others.

If your pony must be stabled for long periods of time:

◆ Use a stable where he can see plenty of activity and other horses.

◆ Feed plenty of hay.

◆ Use a haynet with small holes so it takes longer to be emptied.

◆ Split feed into several meals. Visit as often as possible.

◆ Exercise for at least 1-1/2 hours a day, if possible, divided into more than one ride throughout the day.

◆ Check that he is not being bullied by the next-door pony.

◆ Give him a stable toy, such as a horseball, to play with.

◆ Play soft, quiet music.

it's a fact!

In every pony's brain is the exact number of chews he knows he ought to have each day to take in the right amount of food. If he is on schedule, he can relax. If his body and brain tell him he should be eating more, yet there is no food to chomp on, he can get anxious. This happens with many stabled horses. It is also the reason why many ponies in lush pastures go on eating long after they cannot possibly be hungry!

Above: Whenever a pony is stabled, make sure he has plenty of hay to occupy his digestion for as long a time as possible.

Above: Stable toys, like this horseball, give a horse something to think about.

The herd

Below: Whether they are racehorses or school horses, all groups of horses act as herds.

To a pony, being part of a herd is more than just hanging around with a bunch of pals or even growing up with a family. Once again, it is all about survival.

Sticking together in a group has its advantages. First and foremost, there is safety in numbers. More individuals means there is less chance of anyone being picked off by a predator. Less danger means more eating time. When it comes to searching out food and water, several noses are always better than one. What is more, the herd is just the place to find an ideal mate.

The herd in your field

What do wild herds have to do with the ponies people ride? The answer is — everything!

really wild facts

How big is a herd in the wild?
It can be as small as two horses or as large as twenty. Most herds have about eight to ten members. The herd includes one mature stallion, several mares, and their youngsters up to about the age of two.

What does the stallion do?
All the horses know the stallion is the top male. He spends most of his time organizing and protecting his family. In a crisis, he is much more likely to be somewhere at the back, rounding up the vulnerable

A stallion uses a head-down, driving motion to move the herd along.

stragglers, than leading the escape. He saves his aggression for any direct challenges to his authority from a younger male — and then it's no holds barred!

Are all the mares equal in status?
No, there is usually one "boss" mare that calls the shots, not only among the other mares, but the entire herd. Even the stallion will often take his lead from this experienced matriarch. She is usually the one to decide when

An experienced mare makes most of the decisions for the herd.

to move on and when to settle. She acts as the pathfinder, and she puts misbehaving youngsters in their place. The other mares may have foals or be barren (not pregnant with a foal).

Do youngsters stay with the herd?
In the wild, foals are weaned gradually as their mother prepares for her next baby. Fillies then stick around for another year or so. Then, they usually drift away to join a group of young males or are claimed by a stallion.

Young males have a tougher time because as they mature, they become a threat to their sire, or father. At about eighteen months old, they are driven away and form "bachelor" herds. A particularly strong, young stallion may eventually challenge an older one for his herd, or claim any young fillies in the area and start a herd of his own.

Are horse families close?
Family bonds between horses are very strong, although we rarely get the chance to see this in domesticated horses. Even after another foal is born, youngsters will graze, run, and socialize with their mothers and other close relations.

Have you ever noticed that every time a group of horses or ponies gets together, before you know it, they are acting like a herd? Whether it is in a field, in a stable yard, at a lesson, or at the racetrack, it doesn't take long to see that horses and ponies prefer to be together, rather than going it alone. Although there is usually one horse that enjoys being leader, most horses in a group like to follow.

Horses cannot help behaving as if they are in a herd. This is very obvious by watching their behaviors in a field. Even in a row of stables, however, there will be some horses snoozing but always one acting as a "look-out" — up and on the alert for danger. Outdoors, if something spooks one pony, in an instant the entire herd will be galloping off together as if their lives depended on it.

Within a domesticated herd, there will be bossy ponies and shy ponies, friends and enemies too, just as there are in a herd of wild mustangs. These relationships help bond the herd together and make it a living, ever-changing society.

Living together

What makes a herd operate so well is that it is built on friendship, harmony, and working together. What could be more risky for a prey animal than for the group to be distracted by constant squabbling, resulting in wasted energy and injuries?

Horses understand cooperation. They are not naturally aggressive and rarely go looking for a fight. This is something we must try to remember when we are dealing with them and things do not go according to plan. The reason horses get along so well with humans is that they usually want to please us.

What about a pecking order?

Many people still have the idea that groups of horses always have a strict hierarchy, or pecking order. They think there is a bully at the top that gets all the best food and gives the orders, with another pushy character as second-in-command, and the rest of the group all lined up below,

with the weakest or most timid at the bottom — the one who always gets bossed around. If an animal wants to go up in status in this kind of society, he would have to challenge the one above him on the ladder.

In fact, horse herds in the wild do not work that way at all. It makes no sense for individuals to be fighting all the time when there is plenty of food and space for everyone.

The only time a type of status order does develop and the arguments start is when there is competition for something scarce that all the horses want. This rarely happens in the wild, but it is seen quite often in domesticated horses. Ponies in a field will graze happily together until you take a bucket of feed out. Then you soon see who is "top dog!"

Above: A pecking order only shows itself within a group of horses when individuals are given something to fight about, like a bucket of feed.

Friendly relations

Although horses tend to get along well and do not make an issue out of status, this does not mean that each individual gets along equally well with all his herd-mates. Watch a group of ponies in the field to see which ones are friends and which ones would rather not "talk" to each other. Friends graze close together or maybe even stand nose-to-tail, swishing flies away from one another's face or indulging in a bit of mutual grooming by nibbling one another's neck and crest. A pony that dislikes or feels intimidated by another pony will keep well out of the way.

An individual pony's own personality affects the way he fits in with the rest of the group. Shy characters feel vulnerable, and they tend to stick with and befriend other tolerant, easy-going ponies. Bullyish or grumpy characters tend to stand alone in the group. These types of characters are rarely the real bosses, though. The ponies in charge are confident and popular and like making decisions. This is the type of character that gives a nervous pony or rider confidence, perhaps by giving a lead over a fence. Which type of character is your four-legged friend?

Personal space

Do you feel comfortable in a crowd if someone stands right in front of you? Most animals have a strong sense that the space immediately around them is theirs. They feel threatened if another animal comes too close without being invited.

Although horses do not like being too far away from each other, they also want their individual space. This distance varies between ponies, often according to how confident, grumpy, or submissive each character is. It is usually around 6.5-10 feet (2-3 m).

Friends may be allowed very close. Disliked individuals are warned off with a threatening facial expression or a leg lifted, ready to kick. A stranger is expected to ask permission with an outstretched nose and an exchange of sniffs before he steps closer.

Beyond a pony's personal distance is a slightly wider area called the "flight" distance. If he does not want to deal with a pony that encroaches in this area, he simply walks or runs away — as anyone who has a pony knows!

Ponies living with humans get used to us barging in on their personal space without asking permission, particularly when they are stabled. Next time you approach a pony, remember your manners. Come up lightly and see what his reaction is. Then, introduce yourself before intruding where you may not be welcome.

Above: If one pony intrudes on another's space, he will either be warned off or will move away himself, depending on how assertive he is.

Above: Many ponies get touchy and grumpy in the stable because they don't have the choice of moving away when someone unwelcome invites themselves in.

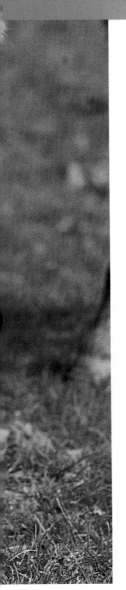

Above: Sometimes a twosome can get too dependent on each other, leading to problems. If your pony has a special friend, try to make sure the two are parted regularly for short spells.

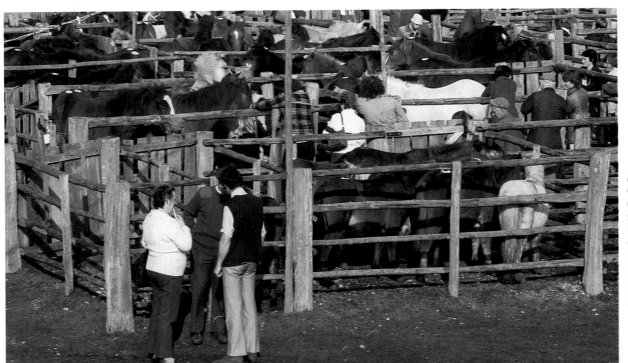

Left: Over-crowding can be as stressful as being without companions. Crowded horses and ponies get nervous about their space.

Pony talk

Horses and ponies "talk" to each other and to us all the time. Despite not being able to speak, horses still have a very expressive language. They communicate with body signals.

Some pony talk is very obvious and easy to understand. Other messages are more subtle. Take time to listen, and you will find your pony has plenty to say. By learning to translate what he is saying and getting on your pony's wavelength, you will be well on your way to becoming the best of friends.

Ways of communicating

Every part of a horse's body is used for communication, either individually or as a segment of a bigger, overall picture. Smart riders will be able to translate what their pony is trying to tell them by carefully watching his body language.

body business

As you can see from the photographs on this page, the outline of the body communicates a great deal about what a horse or pony is thinking and feeling.

tops and tails

Ears and tails give signals, and they often work together. Tail up means excitement, alarm, or interest. Tail down means sleepiness or perhaps discomfort. A horse or pony that is afraid flattens his tail as much as he can. A lashing or swishing tail often indicates annoyance or discomfort.

Floppy ears are simply relaxed. However, droopy, stiff ones may be a sign a pony himself is feeling "down" for some reason. Neutral ears sit slightly forward, but when there is something intriguing happening, the ears point in that direction to find out more. Ears flicking back and forth means the pony is not quite sure where to focus his attention or that he is worried. Ears back always means trouble. An annoyed pony's flattened ears mean, "Caution, steer clear." A frightened or galloping pony will also press his ears backward in order to protect them.

Above: As a rule, the more excited or alarmed a pony is, the more alert and eye-catching everything about him is. With his tail in the air, head high, ears pricked, his muscles are tight with tension and his steps are prancing, ready for action. This mood is very infectious for the other ponies, and they join in!

Above: In contrast, a low, smooth, relaxed outline and unhurried movements say there is nothing of interest going on. A droopy outline does not always mean a happy, sleepy pony though. One that is dejected, submissive, or in pain may also be droopy, but he would stand still for long periods with his head hanging down, a tense expression, and tail tucked in.

Above: Sometimes horses use whole-body movements, often when they are being defensive. Swinging the back end around and perhaps lifting a leg is a warning to another pony (or person) to back off. Horses generally prefer to present a threat first, rather than launch into a full-scale attack.

it's a fact!

Zebras, donkeys, showjumping horses, and your pony all speak the same language, which is millions of years old. In contrast, humans have hundreds of different languages. No wonder horses get along with each other better than we do!

tip

Prey animals are incredibly sensitive to signs of tension. Horses interpret stiffness and jerkiness in other horses or in humans as a warning sign of danger. Try to stay relaxed, and move carefully but confidently around ponies so as not to send the wrong message.

Above: A frightened pony can easily panic. Fear makes his entire body stiffen. With a tense neck, the pony rolls his eyes wide to see what is behind him. The ears are flat back. The mouth is set and nostrils flared to take in as much air and scent as possible for a quick exit.

I wonder what . . .

ponies talk about. They express their moods and feelings, just as people do! Horses can be happy, interested, bored, frightened, frustrated, angry, or miserable. However, they generally feel this way for different reasons than people do.

Above: Stiff, droopy ears can be a sign a pony is feeling "down."

Above: A lashing or swishing tail means the pony is annoyed or irritated at something.

Drawn-back lips can mean angry aggression, but not always. This little foal is "mouthing" at an older horse. He is saying "Look at me. I'm big and tough!"

Making faces

Horses cannot quite get the detailed expressions on their faces that people can. However, they are able to communicate many things with the lips, nose, and eyes. One of the most dramatic facial expressions is, of course, the flehmen action.

By a head

Assertive ponies will often make an upward jerk of the head. This might be followed with an angry lunge at a companion. A gentle nudge of the nose is a way of asking for some attention or a treat. Shaking or tossing the head or neck is often done in annoyance.

Legging it

Besides giving a general impression of how a pony is thinking and feeling, leg movements carry their own meanings, too.

Stamping is usually a mild protest. A pony will stamp out of annoyance, perhaps at flies or when his girth is being fastened. Pawing the ground shows impatience.

Although resting a hind foot is normal for a relaxed pony, drawing the foot up sharply is a warning to, "Keep your distance, or I'll kick!" Striking out with a foreleg is a very aggressive action usually only seen between loose horses that have a serious problem with one another. A pony that strikes out with a foreleg really means business.

tip

If your pony regularly behaves aggressively, get help before a dangerous situation develops.

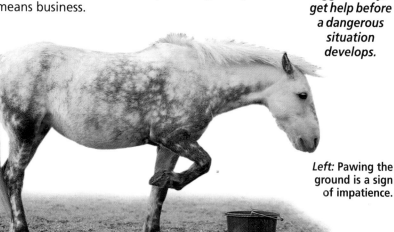

Left: Pawing the ground is a sign of impatience.

Above: Eyes can be wide with alertness, concentrating hard on something of interest. Or they might have a faraway, contented look or be almost closed with exhaustion or pain. Angry eyes roll back and bulge.

Above: Fear or worry creates a pinched muzzle that is tight with tension. In contrast, a relaxed or tired pony has soft nostrils and a saggy, loose muzzle and lips. Noses wiggle in playfulness or wrinkle up in irritation, disgust, or discomfort.

I wonder why . . .

horses developed a language based on sight, not sound.

Vocal communication would have alerted predators to the whereabouts of the herd. For an animal living in a group in an open environment, subtle and almost silent visual clues were more effective.

talking "pony"

Practice talking to your pony in his own language! It's amazing how much he will pick up from your movement and actions if you imitate the way horses communicate with each other. Here are some expressions to try:

On the offensive Use this to warn off an aggressive or bullying pony, to turn loose ponies away from you, or as a reprimand for misbehavior in the field or stable (do not do it too enthusiastically when the pony is tied up). Stand in front of the pony. Look him straight in the eye, raising your elbows up slightly, away from your body.

Submissive Use this to entice a pony toward you, to make friends, or to reassure a pony that you are nothing to worry about. Relax and take slow, deep breaths. Let your hands hang down at your sides. Drop your shoulders, and look at the ground. Turn your body at an angle to the pony's shoulder. All this is saying that you are not a threat.

Take an aggressive stance if you want a pony to back off from you.

A droopy posture, with eyes downcast, gives a nonthreatening message

who's calling?

Horses and ponies have other ways of communicating besides their special "sign language." Horses may not use their voices as much as people do, but they can express many different moods and messages through calls.

Neigh or whinny
A long, loud call used to make contact or identify another pony.

Snort
A snorting pony opens his nostrils up, drawing in plenty of air, ready for action. Snorts are often alarm signals, warning of danger.

Nicker
This soft, low sound is welcoming. Stallions use a long, deep nicker with a mare they like. The mare's quiet nicker to her foal tells him she is concerned, so please stay close.

Squeal
This is a loud, close-range warning or indignant protest for others to stay clear. The exception is a mare in a playful mood with a stallion.

Scream
Horses don't roar like lions, but they do make a raw, high-pitched scream in the wild when emotions run high.

Grunt
A pony will sometimes grunt when he is getting up from the ground or when yawning.

Sigh
Like humans, ponies tend to sigh when they are tired, bored, or irritated.

Nose blow
A hearty "nose blow" is a sign that a horse or pony is at ease with life.

When you feed hay to ponies in the field, put out more piles or safely tied nets than there are ponies, or the shy feeders will never get their fair share.

Ponies and people

Above: Bring ponies in to give them concentrate feeds. When ponies eat at the same time, separate them at least 10 feet (3 m) apart.

By getting into the habit of seeing life through your pony's eyes, you will find that there are suddenly many different ways, large and small, that you can get along better together.

On the loose

Ponies loose in a field or other large space will act like a mini-herd. Although individuals will rarely be deliberately aggressive to a human, a group of ponies often gets carried away with little rivalries and jealousies among them. It would be easy for you to get caught in the middle! Always be on the watch for trouble.

Be careful to never take a single feed bucket into a field because this is guaranteed to cause a riot with possible injuries as a result. Slip a piece of apple or carrot into your pocket, instead. Give the special treat to your pony as a reward for letting himself be caught.

Going solo

Horses always feel most secure and settled with others around them. It takes quite a bit of confidence and trust in you — his human friend — for a pony to be perfectly happy going out without the others.

You will notice that whenever a pony is unsure, worried, or even simply having a difference of opinion with you, he will move toward other horses for moral support. Sometimes it can turn into a very awkward habit called "napping," when the pony might refuse to go forward.

This magnetic attraction is very strong in ponies and is something to be aware of in many situations. It can work for or against us. On the plus side, it gives a nervous pony confidence by finding him an experienced friend to ride with. A field-mate can provide companionship to a worried new arrival. On the other hand, there is a problem if a pony is convinced he must always have a companion in every situation.

Boost your pony's trust in you and his confidence to do things without the others. Don't always ride out with others — go out by yourself sometimes, too. On trail rides with friends, switch the order in which you ride. Try several different activities with your pony, and take him out as much as possible.

Be flexible and sensible about when to keep him away from others and when to allow him the extra reassurance of horse companionship. For example, you can expect a pony left on his own in a field to gallop around neighing and looking for his friends. If you don't want him to get upset or the field to be chewed up, provide another pony to keep him company. If your pony is reluctant to load into a trailer, decide whether putting another pony in first will be a help or whether he will concentrate better out of all sight and earshot of others.

There are no hard-and-fast rules, but taking a pony's eye view of each situation will help you make a decision on how best to operate.

First impressions

As far as a pony is concerned, objects creeping up on him are bad news. If a pony is taken by surprise, we cannot blame him if he is startled, jumps forward, steps on someone's foot, pulls the lead rope from your hands, or even bucks. These are purely instinctive actions, and it would be unfair to punish your pony for responding in this way. It is up to us to always give warning that we are near. When you approach a stall door or come close to a pony that is tied up, say

his name and wait a moment to give him time to turn and see you. Hold out a hand and stroke or rub his neck.

As you can imagine, ponies do not like abrupt, jerky actions like your running around or arm-waving. Loud, raucous noise and shouting frightens them and puts them on edge. They are also worried by nervous, tense movement and touches by people. A pony will sense if you're scared, but it is unlikely he will realize that you are frightened of him! Alternatively, if a bossy pony encounters a nervous rider or handler, he can quickly decide to take advantage and try to get his own way with everything.

To make a pony feel at ease, we must be relaxed, quiet, and confident around him. Be considerate of his feelings, and remember how sensitive he is, especially to sudden movements and sharp sounds.

Learn to trust each other. Good handling of your horse or pony involves getting him to do what you want — without making him afraid.

it's a fact!
...that with the help of his wide field of vision, a pony can actually see the rider on his back.

Above: Be relaxed and confident around a pony. Make sure he always knows where you are, so you don't startle him.

Above: When a pony with a strong character has met a rider that is timid or vague with her aids, he soon learns to take advantage.

Left: Boost a pony's confidence by riding with a steady, reliable companion. Don't let him get too used to always having an equine friend, however.

Free & easy

Catching a horse or pony involves common sense. Approach him in a courteous manner. Remember, it's understandable for a horse or pony to be suspicious if you appear from an angle where he cannot see you — that is, from behind him or from directly in front. Walk calmly toward his shoulder, hesitating when you get near to allow him to look around to see better if he wants to.

By keeping the halter at your side, you aren't sending out any cause for alarm. Speak softly. There is no need to shout — horses have excellent hearing. Hold out your hand as a welcome. Loop a lead rope around his neck first. Then quietly put the halter on.

Pick the right moment for catching your pony and putting on his halter. Conditions should be calm and relaxed. It is not a good time to catch him if all the occupants of the field have just been excited by a new arrival, if there is some fascinating activity going on nearby, or if there is stormy, windy weather in the air. Let things settle down a little first.

It may also be helpful to bring some of his companions in at the same time. That way he won't feel as though he is the only one that has to stop playing and go home.

Above: Get into the habit of making your pony stand still before releasing him.

a good catch

When catching a pony, loop the lead rope around the neck first to give you something to hold him with. Putting the halter on first gives him every chance to move away before you're ready.

Have a treat, such as a piece of carrot or apple, in your pocket to reward your pony when he is caught. Taking a bucket into a field of horses or ponies could cause a dangerous riot.

I wonder why...

my pony leans into me when I lean on him. It is often thought that horses move away from pressure, whereas, in fact, they move into any prolonged pressure. This is a natural survival instinct that would lessen damage in an attack. If a wounded horse pulled away from the jaws of a predator, he would be badly injured. If, however, he went "with" the bite and waited an instant for the attacker to relax its grip, the horse might be able to escape.

get knotted

- Always use a quick-release knot and tie up to a loop of twine rather than directly to the ring or fence.

- Never tie up to an object that is not stationary (like an open gate or something lying around the yard).

- Never tie a pony up by his reins. If he pulls back, you will have an expensive tack repair bill.

- Don't leave a tied-up pony alone, not even for a minute. He is not a parked car!

- If you have a friend with you, ask her or him to hold your pony rather than tie him up, especially if the pony needs reassurance — like when the vet or farrier visits. Many ponies get panicky if they feel too restricted.

Right: **Ponies that are tied up feel restricted. If they are startled, they could panic.**

Above: **A pony's feet are his most precious possessions — treat them with care and respect.**

Brush strokes

Grooming should be relaxing for you both and an opportunity to get to know each other better. Try to use bold strokes. Be aware of places where a pony is particularly sensitive. Always start at the top of the neck and work down the body rather than launching straight into areas where all ponies feel more touchy, like under the belly or on the legs. Most will have ticklish spots where they dislike being brushed. Use a softer brush or just your fingers on those areas.

When it comes to picking out the feet, stand close by the pony's side, and make sure he is standing with his weight on all four legs before you start. Run your hand firmly down the leg and give a little tug to the fetlock to ask him to lift the foot. If he ignores the request, lean into him and give a little nudge (not a sharp poke!) just behind the elbow. This will make him shift his weight slightly off that foot.

Don't hold the foot too high or expect your pony to keep it up for a long time because this is uncomfortable. Put it down carefully — you may be accidentally kicked if he is allowed to wave it in the air.

The right way to ask

Ponies feel happiest when you make it clear what you want from them.

Make commands firmly but also be kind and reasonable. If, for example, you want your horse or pony to move over in the stable, put a hand flat against his side. With a very definite, but not prodding, nudge, say a confident "Over!" Whenever you want a pony to move a few steps sideways or backward, give the same short, firm nudge or push. Don't lean into him — he will only lean back.

Talk to your pony using commands that are easy for him to learn to recognize. Your pony will not understand the words, but if you use them consistently, on the same occasions with the same tone of voice, he will come to know what you want. You may want to use his name first, but then keep it short and simple, like "Patch, back!", "Walk on!", or "Whoaaa." Avoid hiding the request in a complete sentence, such as, "Patch, if you wouldn't mind just taking a couple of steps backward, I'd be really grateful." This is extremely polite, but your pony will have no idea what you are talking about.

tip

First, pick up the foreleg the pony has farthest back, then the hind leg on the same side and work around. In this way, he can easily rebalance his weight.

Below: **From this position, you could get kicked. Stand to the side, facing the tail.**

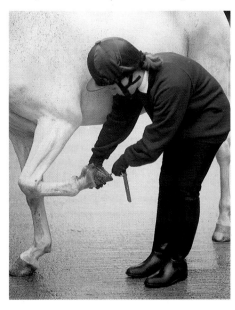

Taking the lead

Below: A pony should walk quietly just alongside or slightly behind you.

Horses are natural followers, so most will walk happily alongside or just behind you. If you want to encourage an anxious or nervous pony, walking just ahead of him will be the most effective way of encouraging him. Do not turn to face him or try pulling him along.

Avoid holding onto the halter itself or having the rope too short because most horses will fight against this. About 10 inches (25 cm) away is good, with the slack end of the rope in your other hand, not dragging along the ground where the pony could step on it and frighten himself.

Another big mistake would be to wrap the lead rope around your hand. Anything could startle and panic your pony, and you could be dragged.

Independently minded characters will often try to take the lead themselves. Remind your pony who's in charge with a firm, sharp tug on the lead rope.

It is very dangerous to have a pony running around wherever he pleases, dragging you with him.

Teach a pony to lead quietly and calmly. If you both are good at this, you both will be successful because it is the basis of almost all handling. If you have problems with this, it says your pony has very little respect for humans and would rather do as he pleases.

We all know that in a contest of strength, ponies could win hands (or hooves) down every time. The secret of good handling is to never let them realize this!

Above: Always put a bridle on for extra security when on a road.

Sloppiness causes accidents.

Above: The arrival of a newcomer is always an exciting event.

Above: Give a new arrival time to safely get to know the others.

Above: If two horses don't get along, separate them.

Making friends

The arrival of a new pony is always a big event for all the ponies. Strangers are greeted with curiosity, but caution. Accidents often happen when people rush the introductions.

Help a new arrival settle in by stabling him next to a quiet, inoffensive character first so that he can make a friend. Ride him out with the other horses so they all have a chance to sniff each other. Don't expect to jump on and ride him all day. Give him an opportunity to take in his new surroundings and relax a little.

Adding a new personality will always unsettle a group for a while and set up a new web of relationships, so expect adjustments to take a while. It is unfair to turn a new pony out into a group of others that all know each other because they are sure to see him as an intruder. Turn him out with his reliable friend first, adding other ponies gradually until they are all on friendly terms.

Getting along

As a rule, be careful about standing ponies too close to each other, even out riding. Do not forget they like their personal space. If they know each other well, fine. If they are strangers, you never know quite what is going to happen. A squeal, grumpy face, or even a kick is quite likely.

If a pony is being bullied by the others in a field, try putting different combinations together and separating him from the more aggressive characters until you find a happy mix. A pony that is an underdog in one group may be quite content if just one of the other aggressive horses is taken away. After the change, all the relationships in the group will shift.

Also, remember your pony's friends and not-so-good friends, when it comes to stabling. Putting sworn enemies next door to each other is not a formula for peace and harmony!

Good and bad behavior

How does your pony view you? Does he see you as his friend, his family, or his leader? A good partnership is usually a mix of all these things, but the common ingredient is that the two of you trust and respect each other. Gaining your pony's respect is not about showing him who's boss. It's about being on the same team, with you as captain.

Friendship — the best reward

To show a horse or pony affection, rub or scratch him on the neck or crest. This is how horses and ponies show friendship among themselves. A rub or scratch cannot be misunderstood, whereas a pat can seem to be a slap or a nervous tickle.

In a quiet moment, your pony might lean over your shoulder or put his head into your chest. Don't push him away or be upset. He is just treating you like another pony and asking for a scratch and a cuddle!

Remember, ponies cannot see very well directly in front of their faces, so never suddenly bring up a hand to pat a pony between the eyes.

Treats are another way of saying hello or well done, but don't overdo them. A pony that comes to expect one every time you put a hand in your pocket can soon get bad-tempered and learn to nip. Keep treats for special occasions and when you catch him or say good-bye.

Ponies behaving badly

Ponies know all about discipline. Every herd member learns to respect those in authority. Horses like rules and having someone in charge.

When we ask horses to live in our human herd, we must help them feel safe and at ease. For our two species to get along well together, humans must take on the role of herd leaders. This means we set the rules, give rewards for good behavior, and provide discipline when rules are broken.

As long as the rules are reasonable and considerate, this is fair. After all, no one would end up the winner if your pony ran the show. As long as he is living with humans, his resources are limited by us.

Above: Ponies appreciate a rub on the neck far more than a pat because it is a friendly gesture they understand.

Below: If you come up against a pony problem, don't let the situation get serious. Ask for advice.

Awkward customers

Occasionally, you may come across a pony that is particularly awkward or misbehaved, despite all your best efforts. In this case, ask your instructor or another experienced horse person for advice. Don't struggle with the situation until it gets to be a real problem. It takes skill and experience to recognize the difference between a stubborn pony that is testing you and one that may have a genuine excuse for his behavior. In the latter case, it is time to call in an expert. Some problems are best handled only by the professionals.

Above: A treat is one way of making friends. Be careful how you give one. Scrunching your fingers up like this could lead to them being munched by mistake! Keep the hand flat. Don't overdo treats, or he will expect them.

some simple rules

Your pony cannot read your mind

Your pony has no idea what your intentions are or why you are asking him to do some strange or unnatural (from his viewpoint) things. It is up to you to teach him what you want. Do this by being clear about what you expect.

Be fair and consistent

Ponies learn quickly when a situation is black and white but are easily confused if things are forever shifting. Don't let him get away with bad behavior one day, but not the next. Just because you're in a bad mood one day, don't take it out on him. Set rules and stick to them, so he always knows where he stands. He will appreciate this because that is his nature.

Think and react quickly

If your pony oversteps the mark, let him know immediately. Depending on the horse's character and what he has done wrong, this may be with a stern "No!" Never smack a horse or pony around the head or jab his mouth with the rein.

Whether you are disciplining or praising him, you must do it within three seconds or he will not connect his action with your reaction. It is no use disciplining him minutes later out of frustration or to punish him. Discipline instantly, then put it behind you. Try to show him what you wanted so he knows how to do it right the next time. When he does well, praise him immediately so he knows he did it correctly.

Be committed, convincing, and in control

Your pony needs to know you mean it so don't be half-hearted, but be fair, too. Anyone who loses her temper with a pony has no understanding of the way a pony's mind works.

Insist on good behavior

Many pushy ponies will enjoy seeing how much they can get away with, and some might become stubborn about wanting their own way. As long as you are sure you are not asking for anything unreasonable, don't give up too easily. Keep on insisting. If you are not persistent, it won't take long for a stubborn character to recognize a pushover when he sees one!

Above: When your pony does well, praise him immediately so he knows he has done a good job.

The horse's finely tuned system of balance and coordination is one of nature's miracles.

How smart is your pony?

Many books about riding and pony care and even instructions from your riding teacher make it sound as if you just have to press some buttons and your horse or pony will do what you want. Of course, horses and ponies are not machines. They have minds and wills of their own.

Misunderstandings often happen between humans and horses because we expect them to think and react in exactly the same way we do. Ponies have a different view and different priorities than us, however. Their minds also work quite differently from ours. Learning about how your pony thinks and feels will help you understand why those buttons don't always work.

Above: Horses probably have as great a range of emotions as humans. However, they don't spend a lot of time thinking about their emotions as humans do.

Above: Humans evolved as hunters, outwitting their elusive prey. So our brains became good at solving problems and weighing possibilities. In contrast, all a prey animal like a horse needed to know was how to escape danger.

pony brains make them good at:

♦ Balance and coordination. Horses have a large cerebellum, where locomotion and muscle coordination are centered.

♦ Sensory perception. All the areas that control senses are very well developed.

♦ Feelings. The limbic system deep in the middle of the brain controls emotions. This is just as large and complicated in horses as in humans, suggesting that horses have as wide a range of emotions as humans, and feel them just as strongly.

pony brains are not geared for:

♦ Analyzing feelings.

♦ Imagining or thinking creatively.

♦ Understanding situations.

♦ Solving problems.

♦ Planning for the future.

Masterminds

Most of a horse's brain is taken up with survival thinking — there is not much spare space for the luxury of contemplating the meaning of life!

The big difference

Reasoning power is the big difference between the way horses and ponies view the world and the way humans view it. Horses and ponies have strong feelings but cannot think about them. In contrast, people spend most of their time thinking about feelings and situations, making plans, and using experiences to solve problems.

Can you imagine living every moment in the present like your pony does — simply reacting to each situation as it comes along — by instinct? No wonder humans handle life differently, and no wonder ponies get so easily stressed if they are kept or ridden the wrong way. In whatever way a pony deals with his feelings, we should always be considerate and respect him.

Are horses intelligent?

Things that horses and ponies are exceptional at are the things humans are not as good at. The things ponies are not good at are exactly what make people think we are so fantastic!

Because horses and other animals are not great "thinkers" and seem to react to things blindly, they are often incorrectly labeled with the awful word *dumb*. There are many times a horse must view humans as a bit dense, such as when we are not as fast, observant, or sensitive as he is. In fact, it is hardly right to think of a horse as unintelligent when we expect him to adapt to our way of living, figure out what we want, and then try to get it right all the time. Yet we ourselves make little attempt to learn *his* language!

I wonder why . . .

my instructor always makes me repeat an exercise in both directions. Like ours, a horse's brain is split into two hemispheres. Humans apply something that has been learned on one side of the body to the other side, but horses do not. For horses and ponies to learn thoroughly, you must go over each exercise in both directions.

The problem with intelligence is deciding how to measure it. How do we compare two vastly different species and then compose an examination that is fair? Each animal is perfectly tuned to his own natural surroundings. Put him in a new and strange environment and, of course, many of his reactions are inappropriate. So the animal sometimes seems clumsy and out of place. Horses would not have made it this far if they had not been intelligent regarding the skills they needed to survive. Horses and ponies don't make great humans, but they are unsurpassed at being brilliant horses and ponies!

hands down

A lot of human accomplishment comes down to the fact that we have hands, when a pony is stuck with just hooves! If we have a problem, our hands give us many options to solve it. In comparison, a pony can only run or possibly fight.

Above: Horses are very adept at finding ways around the limitations of having only hooves. When you feel like a scratch, ask a friend.

What are ponies good at?

Pony talents are tailored to a pony's world — super senses, amazing coordination, and lightning reactions. Here are some other skills that color your pony's outlook on the world.

Wait a minute…

Just as they are sensitive to the slightest signs in body language, horses notice other details around them, too. These might include a new road sign along the route you usually ride, a cat sitting in the field, and a field-mate with a different blanket on. Go into the field wearing a strange hat, and see what happens.

Horses are suspicious of even tiny changes because it would be too risky for a hunted animal to always presume that everything is okay. A horse judges every situation thoroughly.

Jumping a few logs in the woods does not mean your pony is prepared for cross-country, where he might come across ditches and traps. Years of jumping a variety of obstacles, however, helps the horse sail over most anything. His rider has trained him to generalize that there is a safe landing ahead, even if it cannot be seen.

Above: Horses are aware of every detail of their surroundings. They are suspicious of any changes.

Difficult decisions

Anything new or strange, however small, always appeals to a pony's curiosity. Often you will see a horse or pony getting quite agitated because he wants to investigate something further but feels nervous and is on his guard in case the object in question is dangerous. Any situation where he is being pulled in different directions by his instincts puts a pony in a dilemma. Horses and ponies have a problem making difficult decisions.

Try this experiment. Give your pony two feed buckets. He will probably switch from one bucket to the other, not sure about which to eat from. A hungry dog, in contrast, is almost certain to polish off one feed bowl without a second thought, before moving on to the next.

Left: All horses and ponies, but particularly youngsters, have a strong sense of curiosity combined with a natural wariness. Horses are often torn between the two impulses and can be easily upset.

it's amazing!

Early in the 1900s, a German called van Osten believed his horse, Clever Hans, could count. Hans wowed audiences throughout Europe with his incredible ability to paw the answer to math problems. One day Hans had to perform in a room where no one knew the correct answers, and he began to get things wrong. All along, Hans had been reacting to the increased tension and unconscious body cues of the audience to reach the correct number.

Talent-spotting

Horses each have their own individual strengths, too, and that's part of what makes riding so interesting. Is the pony you ride emotional and sensitive, or is he laid back?

Some breeds and types tend to have particular personalities and suit particular types of riders. Within every breed, individuals can be especially smart or talented, too.

Some competition riders like to have a horse that can think for himself to get out of a tight spot. However, the horse might be too smart about avoiding what he doesn't like. Others prefer a horse that will always do as he is told and that relies on his rider. Then what happens if the rider makes a mistake? Which type of horse would you prefer?

Personality counts in performance as much as a horse or pony's physical characteristics. A confident character that loves a challenge and lives in the fast lane would make a brilliant competition horse but would be disastrous for teaching novice riders.

Above: Horses are easily confused and worried by vagueness. They like things to be precise. In your riding, particularly with a young horse, don't be wishy-washy with your aids. Clear and definite signals are always appreciated. A horse is never happy about having to make a guess.

A trained dressage horse has learned to tell the difference between hundreds of minute signals given by his rider.

Shy characters, the followers of the herd, would be happy in a riding school or going on a trail ride. Nervous types do better with one owner in a small yard and would hate to be a competition horse traveling to a different show every week.

Most horses seem to enjoy activities like jumping and endurance. Things that don't come very naturally — like going around in circles — aren't always so appealing.

Not all horses can be superstars. But like us, with a good education, they can do some of everything and may be very good at certain things. Try to find your pony's talents and make the most of them.

Don't push your pony to continue with an activity he clearly does not enjoy because you are never going to have fun or succeed at it. Stick to what he is good at. Maybe someday you'll meet a horse that loves exactly the same things you do and does them well!

the right team

Riders and ponies need characters that are suitable for them. If you are a nervous rider, find a pony that gives you confidence but won't take advantage or get upset if you make a mistake.

Most of a pony's early lessons in life come from his mother. Later on, he learns from the group about how to get along with other horses.

How ponies learn

A pony's reactions are very fast and dramatic compared to ours. Even though ponies tend to act instinctively and do not spend time solving problems as we do, they can still learn to control their strong natural reactions and emotions. If horses are to be unafraid of all the strange things we ask them to do, we have to teach them in ways they understand.

Learning is about altering reactions according to your experiences of the past. It can be quite a complicated business, but there are various ways that learning happens.

Getting used to things

One way we teach horses to overcome their natural nervousness is by gradually getting them used to things they are naturally afraid of. This is called habituating. By showing them there is nothing to fear, the instinctive response is reduced. They can then memorize the new experience. For example, they learn that when a saddle is put on, no harm will come to them.

Here are some examples of how this works.

♦ To teach a pony to jump, we start with poles on the ground and little crosspoles — we don't head straight for a 3-foot (1-m) oxer!

♦ When we want a pony to be less nervous walking along a road, we start by walking him past parked cars, then starting the car engines, then driving a car past, then walking out on a quiet road with a companion before heading him out on his own where there might be cars.

♦ A pony is walked through puddles before asking him to cross a stream.

habituation

Habituation is the way horses learn to overcome many of their instinctive fears about what we ask them to do. The more a pony experiences something and he is not harmed, the more he comes to trust the fact that you will not put him in danger. The highly trained police horse is an example of habituation in the extreme.

By breaking the problem down and working on it in small stages, and going over safe ground before asking for a more difficult task, you can help your pony relax.

Habituation can begin the day a foal is born. Some trainers even believe it is best to start carefully handling a foal within hours of the birth. This is called imprint training. Getting a foal used to being handled regularly by humans, and behaving himself from the beginning, gives him a good start to his life with us. It will then be easy for him to accept and understand whatever he is asked to do.

Turn off...

If you had a teacher who kept asking the same question even when you had already given the answer, would you want to keep answering? Wouldn't you start to ignore her?

Many ponies must feel like this when their riders constantly keep banging away at their sides and digging in with their heels, or pulling on their mouths. Overdoing a request without giving any reward or acknowledging the response means the person, or animal, gets too used to it and starts to take no notice.

To keep your pony listening, make your signals short and intermittent, not continuous. When he responds, praise him immediately — this is his reward; he knows he has done the right thing.

Memory

Horses in the wild needed good memories to survive — to remember from year to year where to find water and the best food. This super-memory can be very useful when it comes to training because it means that a horse can learn what we want quickly and thoroughly as long as the lesson is taught well.

The trouble is — if we make a mistake and the pony has a bad experience, he will remember that, too.

Luckily, a lesson generally has to be repeated often before it really sinks in. So as long as we don't keep making the same mistake, all is not lost! However, once a lesson is learned, it really does stick. Then it would take a lot of patient retraining to change. Horses have excellent memories. They can remember a lesson learned long ago, even with no practice in between.

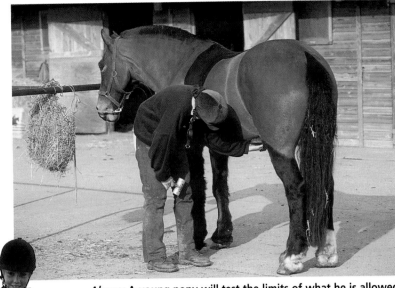

Above: A young pony will test the limits of what he is allowed to do. Handling needs to be kind, but firm, to make sure from the start that everyone knows who is team leader. For example, your pony should not object to your touching him.

Left: When you have given your aid and the pony has responded in any way, do not repeat the aid. Ponies simply tune out if their riders keep giving the same confusing aid. If the pony has not reacted, the aid needs to be better prepared.

I wonder why...

one scare can be enough to put a pony off something for life. Unfortunately, traumatic occurrences (such as a bad fall or accident) stick deeply in a pony's memory. It is very, very difficult to get a pony over this kind of experience. He may always be stressed or panicky about facing the same kind of situation again.

Below: Foals play to develop skills horses need — like spooking at danger, rushing off, and bucking.

Making connections

Getting horses used to situations is their main type of learning. The other way learning takes place is by making connections, or associations. We use this kind of learning, known as conditioning, to teach specific things — like the aids for riding.

It involves linking a signal and a reaction so closely in the mind, that whenever that signal is given, the reaction happens. For example, if you say "whoa" every time you halt and praise him, your pony comes to link the word *whoa* with halt and doing the right thing. Eventually, the word actually comes to mean, "Go slower and stop." So every time you say it, your pony should slow or stop. The more you repeat it, the stronger the habit of stopping becomes. This sort of learning relies on making the pupil want to get it right again, so the connection is made stronger and stronger, which is known as reinforcement.

A good trainer or rider sets everything up so the horse cannot really help but make the right choice. The horse then links that choice with a very obvious signal. When he makes the connection, he is rewarded, so he is more likely to do the same thing next time.

An example:

A rider asks a pony for canter on a curve, so the chances are good that the pony will strike off on the correct leg. If the pony strikes off correctly, the rider praises him and lets him canter on. If not, the request is tried again. The pony soon learns to connect that aid with the right response (striking off on the correct leg) and the reward. Only when a pony has completely understood a lesson can the trainer introduce a more complicated lesson. If she goes ahead too quickly, the poor pony will become more and more confused. For instance, the trainer should make sure the pony knows the aids for halt before worrying about getting him to halt completely square on all four legs. As you can see, training a pony thoroughly takes a lot of time and patience and does not come overnight.

Above: Trainers teach a horse to connect a signal with the response they want by using conditioning. This pony has learned to associate a certain signal from the rider's legs with making a transition to canter.

Trial and error

Even though it is not a very efficient way of learning, we all learn a great deal through trial and error (instrumental conditioning). This also relies on making connections and getting rewards.

Trial and error is the secret behind the training of the world's most advanced horses! It hinges on building understanding little by little. By rewarding the horse whenever he happens to land on the right response to a particular signal, very complicated things are gradually introduced and learned.

An example:

To teach a new movement like half pass (where the horse moves forward and sideways across the arena), the rider gives the leg aid to ask the horse to move over. She ignores a wrong response but praises the horse for even the tiniest movement in the right direction. Once the horse realizes he is doing the right thing, the rider waits for several correct steps before she gives the reward. Step by step, the lesson is built upon. Finally, even very subtly different leg aids come to mean different requests to the horse. It is amazing to think that the most accomplished horses learned by simple trial and error.

During lunging, the horse learns to react to the voice commands of the handler.

Repetition

Whether a lesson is about standing still to be groomed or doing a canter transition, repetition helps forge it into a pony's memory. Don't expect to teach your pony something new in one session — or think he must have learned a new task just because he did it right once.

When a pony has learned something thoroughly, it does usually stick because of his superb memory. Until it is completely understood, however, it needs to be repeated regularly in short lessons with rests in between. Don't expect too much in one session. Praise any progress, and then give your pony a break before he loses patience.

Timing

Good trainers concentrate hard on their responsibilities, especially timing, because it is crucial to get the timing right. For a signal and a reaction to be linked in the pony's mind, these things must happen very close together. There must be instant gratification in order for the pony to connect a reward (or lack of reward) with what he has just done (or not done).

Teaching a pony is no easy task, but timing can lead to success.

Left: Training is built little by little until the horse understands complicated, intricate messages from the rider.

Right: Training a pony is not as easy as it looks. Make your aids as clear as you can. Don't forget, your pony is learning a foreign language.

Below: Make it easy for a horse or pony to get it right. Then reward him immediately.

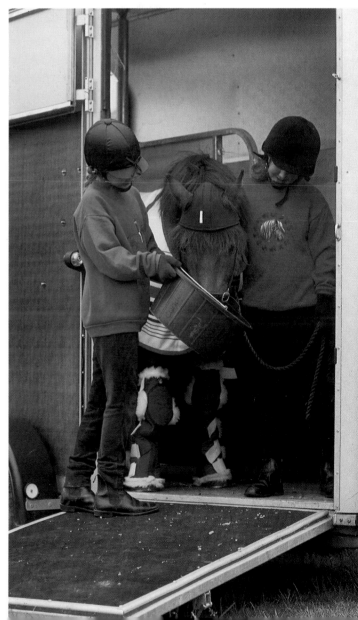

Setting up SUCCESS

Below: You need your pony's full attention if things are to go well.

Learning is easy and fun when lessons are taught well. The advantage you have over a pony is that at least you have some idea of what your teacher at school is trying to show you, what she wants, and why. If you don't understand, you can talk to her and ask her to explain.

Ponies start off not having the faintest idea about what we want from them. Most of what we ask must seem either pointless, or worse, to go completely against their instincts and better judgment. Although they try to tell us this, we don't often listen.

Ponies can't read our minds. When a youngster is taught to lead, how is he to know we won't make him go where there is danger? When it comes to learning to take a rider on their backs, ponies must wonder what on earth is going on.

Overcoming these basic fears is only the first step. We then ask ponies to learn a whole new language — the aids — so they will do what we ask when we are riding them. The world of humans and being ridden must seem very peculiar to a pony. Most of the things we ask him to do he would not dream of doing in his world. It is only fair to try to make it as easy as we can for him to learn what we want, and to make sure he knows how great he is when he gets it right.

Here are some tips to help you achieve success with your pony:

1 attention! Ponies (especially youngsters) often find learning hard work and are easily distracted. To learn, a pony must give his full attention to the task. Pick a quiet time in the yard when there are no diversions. Choose a calm, still day, not a windy one that always gets ponies wound up. Whatever the reason, if he is in an excited or agitated mood, your pony will not be listening to you. Save the lesson for another day.

2 keep cool You both need to be calm and relaxed for things to go well in your lessons. Tension and nervousness will block any chance of achieving what you want.

Owners of flighty ponies or those that get excited at the very sight of jumps will know how hard it is to get them to listen. Young ponies in particular can be just like young children — always on the go, curious, and refusing to sit down.

Above: When your pony is tense, he won't learn. Try to relax and calm him down, or leave the lesson for another day.

Above: If your pony is tense, try to find out why.

On the other hand, if your pony is tense or running around, let him work off some of the energy before asking him to focus and do anything serious.

Don't get upset and punish him just for feeling great or for mistaking what you want. This will only get him more tense and confused, which is guaranteed to make him act up and resist any type of lesson.

Try to be calm yourself. We know horses are good at picking up the slightest signs of tension in the rider or handler. If the rider and handler are edgy or uptight, a horse or pony will get nervous and tense, too. He won't be able to tune in to what he is being asked.

Teach yourself to stay calm and relaxed around your horse or pony, even if things are not going smoothly. Try not to let any annoyance or frustration show. If you are in a bad mood about something, save the schooling for another day. Go for a nice, peaceful trail ride instead.

3 be clear and consistent Remember, ponies like to know where they stand. They get confused and worried if you change the rules.

4 learn to listen Learn to spot the signs of tension building up. Sometimes the cause is easy to spot — he's seen something he wants to look at. Other times you may only notice he is stiff, his mouth is set, and his neck muscles are tight. This is the time to ask yourself why — is it discomfort, worry, or are your aids not clear enough? Whatever the reason, he will not hear your signals until he is relaxed again. Sometimes we are so busy telling ponies the aids, we don't hear what they are saying back!

Don't ask for trouble by overfeeding your pony or keeping him stabled all the time. Ponies have plenty of energy for most things we ask them to do. Even the sleepy characters that try to convince you otherwise have plenty of energy for the tasks at hand. There is no sense in overfeeding — it will only slow him down. In addition, exercise your horse or pony as much as possible to keep him in top form.

Below: Make sure your pony has plenty of opportunities to let off steam!

You probably get nervous at shows, so expect the excitement to get to your pony, too. Allow time to walk around the grounds showing him the sights, which will help you both relax. Show days are not the time for schooling.

Make him want to do it for you!

Learning and being ridden should be fun and easy for your pony. When everyone is feeling positive and confident, progress can be made. When a pony or a rider gets annoyed, everything becomes an uphill battle.

It is important to create the right atmosphere for learning. Increase your pony's motivation by getting on his wavelength.

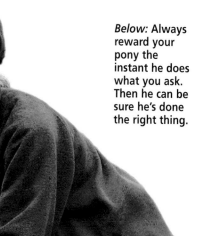

Above: Keep lessons short and simple, tackling one thing at a time. Then give your pony a break.

Depending on the situation, your pony's reward for making the right response could be a gentle rub on the neck, a kind "good boy," or a treat.

Remember, it is crucial that you reward him immediately (within three seconds) or your pony will not associate his action with the pleasant result. When you are riding, a reward could be just relaxing after giving the aid, such as "giving" the reins slightly once he has slowed down or halted, or keeping your heels still once he has stepped it up a notch.

There is nothing like praising your pony to bring you closer together. Teach yourself to ignore mistakes but praise good reactions, however small. You will soon be on your way to becoming a sensitive, caring rider and trainer. It is amazing how many riders are quick to punish their ponies if they get things wrong, but hardly ever mention it when the ponies get things right.

Top: A pony and rider both enjoy lessons that are fun and varied.

Below: Always reward your pony the instant he does what you ask. Then he can be sure he's done the right thing.

To get on his wavelength —

Keep it short
The best lessons are short and to the point. Tension and resistance creep in when ponies get bored or have had enough. Try to finish on a good note.

Make it fun
Don't do the same thing day after day. Challenge and stimulate your pony with many different activities in the ring or out on the trail.

Reward him often
Most of the time, learning relies on rewards. Rewards strengthen the connection between a signal and a response. Rewards make the horse or pony want to repeat the good behavior.

So is punishment wrong? Not always, because ponies are not always angels. They can be deliberately disobedient or stubborn sometimes, and they need to know when their behavior has overstepped the mark, just as they would be told by a "superior" horse in a herd.

Let's look at these situations:

A pony makes a mean face and turns to bite.

The trainer instantly growls at him, squares her body to him, and pushes his head away. He knows displeasure has to do with his intention to bite.

A pony starts to arch his back to buck.

The trainer instantly smacks him behind the girth to drive him forward. The pony knows the smack has to do with his buck.

In these examples, the pony learns to behave. Because the trainer was so quick to respond (remember, praise or discipline must be given immediately — within three seconds), the pony sees the connection between his behavior and the consequences that it created for him.

This is how to prevent problems from developing in the first place. Because the pony has made his own decision, this type of learning lasts. It is extremely important that the trainer be observant, quick to think, and quick to act.

When ponies behave badly, we need to look for reasons. Discovering the causes for the misbehavior often keeps it from happening. Then the problems can be solved before you need to use discipline.

Above: **Be wary of the whip. One quick smack is plenty if you are sure the pony has no excuse for his behavior. Never lose your temper.**

Letting him know when he has it wrong

When a pony makes a mistake, very often it is better to ignore it and then ask again. Make certain you ask clearly and that he is listening properly.

Punishment is designed to link wrong behavior with unpleasantness. But when it comes to ponies, punishment can be full of problems and can easily create fear and misunderstanding.

Learning through punishment makes tense, unhappy ponies. Let's look at three cases:

1 *A pony refuses a jump.* The rider smacks the pony. For the pony to avoid a smack by jumping next time, the smack must happen the instant he refuses, while he is still in front of the fence. Most riders wait a minute, then smack him. No wonder the pony is confused!

2 *A pony bucks and unseats his rider.* She gets back on five minutes later and then jabs him in the mouth. The pony learns that being mounted by a rider is bad. He has no idea that the rider was upset about the earlier buck.

3 *A pony will not be caught.* When the owner finally gets him, she smacks him. He is now convinced that getting caught is bad, because when he does, the rider becomes upset.

Above: **There can be many reasons why a pony stops at a jump — and most of them are the rider's fault.**

Misbehavior checklist

Tackling a problem with your pony is like solving a riddle. Start with these common causes to determine if any of them apply to your situation:

Is it asking the impossible? (or he thinks it is)
...because of asking too much too soon, lack of confidence, asking for something physically impossible, or asking for something illogical (from a pony's point of view).

Is he in pain or discomfort?
...because of tack, sharp teeth, hard ground, injury, stiffness, or bad riding?

Is he stressed or tense?
...because of non-pony-friendly management, too much food, not enough exercise, confusion, being distracted, insecurity, fear, or lack of confidence?

Has he misunderstood?
...because of poor or vague aids, bad timing, or rushed learning?

Is he afraid?
...because of inexperience or a bad experience in the past?

Think what your pony's behavior is telling you.

You may be asking too much.

Cross all of the above off your list of possibilities before concluding that your pony is being just plain naughty. Only then is it time to remind him his behavior is strictly out of order.

Sharp teeth are a common cause of problems.

problem 1
my pony is difficult to lead

What's going on?
A trained pony knows that when there is pressure on the halter, he must move forward alongside the trainer. A pony may not want to move because he is frightened about where he is going. Barging and pushing, however, are sure signs he has found his own strength and is using it.

Your task
If he is worried, overcome his fears.

♦ Remember horses hate dark, enclosed spaces.

♦ Be confident in yourself. Be patient. Reassure him and praise every step forward.

♦ Make sure doors and gateways are wide and high enough so he never frightens himself.

♦ Entice him forward with a treat — this will also keep his head down if he is worried about the height of an entrance.

♦ Don't pull him forward. Have a long schooling whip at your side. As you feel him hesitate, use it gently on his flanks or side. Be careful that he does not jump forward.

♦ Don't hold onto his head too tightly. Horses get worried when they are restricted.

Remind him that you are the one in charge.

♦ Never get relaxed about leading.

♦ Wrapping the lead rope around his nose can help. Use a bridle to lead (and wear gloves) whenever you think extra control may be needed.

♦ If he barges in or out of the stable, place a removable bar across the entrance, so he has to stand calmly before being allowed through.

♦ Every time you feel him starting to rush off when led, say, "Whoa" firmly and prod him in the chest with your elbow. Don't jab him in the mouth or shout at him.

♦ If he starts to pull away, quickly step back at a 45° angle and pull his head around toward you to unbalance him. Don't stand in front of him. When he turns to you, reward him with a slackened rope and praise.

Above: If your pony pulls you around, it's time for some lessons in good manners.

Always wear gloves when handling a pony that is hard to lead or load.

problem 2
my pony won't load

What's going on?
Make doubly sure he has no reason to be afraid before disciplining a pony that is difficult to load. Loading and traveling are stressful for horses. They are naturally claustrophobic. Proper training will help.

Your task
To make this a routine experience that holds no fears.

♦ Have the trailer thoroughly checked for safety.

♦ Drive as if there were a priceless cargo on board — there is.

♦ Make plenty of space inside — don't have partitions too narrow.

♦ Make the trailer inviting. Open all the doors and put down a little bedding.

♦ Position the trailer along a wall to "funnel" the pony in. Park it away from the yard.

♦ Be patient, and keep calm. Allow plenty of time.

♦ Introduce loading lessons to young horses early. Repeat lessons often with short, fun journeys.

♦ Don't crowd the pony with too many helpers.

♦ Don't hold his head too tightly. Lead him calmly toward the center of the ramp.

♦ Entice hesitant ponies with food or a companion. Avoid force. Driving the pony forward from behind with a stick or lunge lines causes resentment and panic. To learn, the pony must choose to go forward himself. Teach very difficult horses with a pressure halter *(see below)*. Praise and reward every step forward.

Above: Think like a pony. Would you walk forward if someone stood right in front of you?

using a *pressure halter*

A pony is a big, strong animal that panics easily. Once he is in the habit of pulling back, barging, or refusing to go forward when led, things can quickly get dangerous. A pressure halter is an effective way of reminding a pony of his manners.

It works by putting pressure on the poll and nose whenever the lead rope tightens, but releasing it when the pony cooperates. He soon learns the comfortable option is best.

Only an experienced handler should work with a halter like this. The handler must keep pressure on the rope whenever the pony misbehaves and release it when the pony gives, stands still, or takes a step forward.

I can't catch my pony

What's going on?

He would rather be free in the field.

Your task

To make him want to be caught.

♦ Don't visit just to ride. Bond with your pony during certain activities, such as grooming.

♦ Always reward him when you catch him.

♦ Check to see if anything is bothering him about riding, such as uncomfortable tack.

Convince him you will get him anyway, regardless of what he does.

First try:

♦ Creating a smaller space to turn him out in, perhaps using high-visibility electric fencing. The odds are in his favor in a large field.

♦ Leaving a halter on (a leather one or one with a quick-release tab) with a short rope that is no more than 7 inches (18 cm) long attached underneath.

♦ Checking that your catching technique is appropriate.

♦ Bringing his companions in. Few ponies like being the odd one out.

Then try:

♦ Walking him down! This is guaranteed to work, but allow plenty of time the first time around. It is based on the advance-and-retreat method used by trainers like Monty Roberts.

Ponies that don't want to be caught can be frustrating.

advance-and-retreat

Using the advance-and-retreat method takes some time and energy but usually gets results that last.

Ponies hate being on their own. The idea behind advance-and-retreat is that you are saying to your pony, "Well, if you want to go away, go on then! But you'll be out there by yourself — and you'll have to stay there."

Walk calmly up to your pony. If he moves away, move with him. Stay within about 15 feet (4.5 m). When he wants to graze, move him on. Keep doing this (without chasing him) every time he stops. After a while, drop your shoulders and turn a few steps away at an angle to him. If he steps toward you, cocks an ear toward you, or drops his head and looks at you, these are signs he is tiring. Eventually, he will turn and let himself be caught.

Trying this in an enclosed area first will help you both get the idea. Always reward a pony when you catch him, however long it has taken. If you punish him, he'll never let you catch him again.

my pony bangs on the stable door

problem 4

What's going on?
He wants to get out! If it only happens at mealtimes, the highlight of his day, it means he cannot wait to get his grub. He wants you to hurry up, and he loves the noise he is making.

Your task
To make his life more interesting and door-banging less appealing.

♦ Turn your pony out more! Door-kicking is a way of saying he is fed up with being in the stall.

♦ Stick to routines. Don't keep your pony waiting for his meals.

♦ Feed all the ponies in the stable at the same time.

♦ If necessary, pad the inside of the door with sacking to dull the noise.

Left: Give me a break! Spending too much time in the stall is at the root of many pony problems.

Left: Always mount carefully, and you won't give a pony any excuse to fidget. Use a mounting block whenever possible.

my pony won't stand still

problem 6

What's going on?
He may be fidgeting because he is uncomfortable. Or he may be so bursting with energy that he can't wait to get going!

Your task
To handle and ride considerately.

♦ Never be rough when handling or tacking up. Move calmly and confidently around your pony. Don't groom ticklish or sensitive places too roughly.

♦ Mount carefully, preferably from a mounting block. Don't poke him in the side with your toe as you get on, or thump onto his back. Adjust stirrups and girths quickly. Check that his saddle and other tack fits well and he does not have a back or tooth problem. Make sure that he is not being fed too much heating food and that he is getting enough exercise and time in the field.

Remind him of his manners.

♦ Keep control. Tie him to a short rope to groom, tack up, etc.

♦ If he moves so much as one step, immediately say a strong "No!" Gently, but firmly, push him back. Don't let yourself become angry.

♦ When mounting, insist he always stand still until asked to move. Say "Stand" or "Whoa."

♦ Reward him when he does well with a rub or a treat.

my pony hates shoeing/water/clipping/traffic

problem 5

What's going on?
This usually begins because a pony is not introduced to these activities carefully or has been frightened by a past bad experience or by being punished for acting worried.

Below: Enlist your farrier's help to overcome the fear of shoeing.

Your task
Reassure your pony.

♦ Introduce ponies (especially youngsters) to new tasks slowly, carefully, and kindly.

♦ Try to see it from a pony's point of view.

♦ Build up in stages, getting the pony used to tiny, unalarming things first before gradually asking for more.

♦ Have other steady ponies around for reassurance.

♦ Be patient and ask the farrier, clipper, and other handlers to keep calm, too.

problem 7

my pony naps

What's going on?
Napping (refusing to go forward) can indicate boredom, tiredness, insecurity, or discomfort.

Your task
Discover which applies.

♦ **Bored/tired.** Keep rides varied and fun by including trail rides as well as schooling. Recognize when he's had enough, especially in a schooling session.

♦ **Insecurity**. *See shying, page 61.*

♦ **Discomfort.** Check out possible reasons for stubbornness, such as discomfort. Be alert to signs of hesitation, and ride strongly. Turn the pony in tight circles, if necessary. Then go on.

Don't let him decide when you are going home. If necessary, sit it out and make sure he gets bored first. Avoid routes that simply go out, turn, and then go back again.

Many ponies bounce and do little half-rears. It is very dangerous when a pony rears full up and means it. Call an expert. If a pony does rear up with you, lean forward up the neck and "give" with the reins.

Above: It is helpful to put a neckstrap on any pony that is likely to shy. An old stirrup leather will do.

Above: Discomfort from tack can be at the bottom of a pony not wanting to go forward. Check the tack thoroughly.

problem 8

my pony can be aggressive (bites/kicks)

What's going on?
A pony that seems to be a bully is actually often worried and insecure. He may have been roughly treated, so has learned to be defensive.

Your task
Don't give him any excuse to be irritated or anxious.

♦ Be considerate and careful in your handling and riding.
♦ Spend time together and build up trust.
♦ Make sure his tack is comfortable.
♦ Give him a lifestyle that is relaxed and friendly. Provide plenty of exercise, and don't overfeed.

Remind him that you are the leader.

♦ Try to stay relaxed and confident.
♦ Remember your body language. Watch carefully. A pony always gives warning signs before striking out, so take notice of them.
♦ A pony will not normally bite or kick unless he feels threatened. Use slow, relaxed movements with downcast eyes and round shoulders when approaching or handling him. Praise him for being good. If he starts to give threatening signs (such as a tight, grumpy face, ears back, swishing tail, a stamping foot), instantly take an aggressive pose yourself (square on, eyes meeting his).
♦ Ponies that bite can be discouraged by fastening a spikey dog brush to your sleeve, so instead of getting a mouthful of you, he gets the brush. Another method is to keep one hand through the halter. Every time he turns his head to nip, jerk it back sharply. Then, immediately, bring it back slowly toward you and rub him gently on the neck or between the eyes. This is telling him — "If you bring your head to me nicely, you will be rewarded."
♦ If you are afraid of a bad-tempered pony, ask an experienced handler to help. This pony may not be suitable for you.

bagging and sacking out

Any pony can be desensitized to sudden sounds and movements with these methods. Ask an adult to help you with bagging. Hang empty, scrunched-up feed bags in the stable. Start with one, and keep adding them so that the pony has to learn to dodge and tolerate bumping his head into them. Bagging is also useful for head-shy ponies. In sacking out, fold up a large plastic sheet and wipe it all over the pony. Take your time and praise him every step of the way. Undo more folds only when he is relaxed about being touched. Continue until the entire sheet is undone and he is okay with it. Don't do more than an hour at a time. If necessary, do it again the next day.

A nervous, jumpy, or head-shy pony is helped by hanging feed bags. He will get used to having them touch his head and appear out of the corner of his eye.

?
problem 9

my pony spooks or shies

What's going on?

Ponies are always on the lookout for danger. They all spook (move quickly sideways) sometimes. Remember how their vision differs from our own. Shying is an instinctive way of moving around to view a strange object better.

Your task

To boost a nervous pony's confidence and keep rides as relaxed and enjoyable as possible.

♦ Introduce a young pony to as many experiences as possible.

♦ Introduce new things gradually. Set up practice situations.

♦ Ride out with a steady companion (but insist he go by himself on quiet, familiar routes sometimes).

♦ Keep relaxed, but alert — don't be caught off guard.

♦ Keep taking riding lessons. A nervous pony needs a positive, effective rider he can trust.

♦ Work on your pony's general schooling so his obedience improves and his attention is on you. Don't let him slop along. Teach him to leg-yield or shoulder-in (ask your instructor about these). You can use these movements to turn his head away from a spooky object. Keep his mind occupied!

♦ Have your whip in your outside hand and use your outside leg to keep his quarters out of the road.

♦ Be patient, and give him plenty of time to have a closer look at anything that worries him.

♦ Never punish or smack a pony for shying.

♦ Try bagging or sacking out (*see panel, page 60*).

♦ Have his eyes checked, just in case there is a problem.

♦ Is he getting enough turn-out time? Is he getting too much of the wrong feed?

Above: Use plenty of outside leg as you go past a "spooky" object to keep your pony from swinging his quarters into the road.

Your pony will soon be ready for anything!

my pony bucks

problem 10

What's going on?
He wants you off his back!

Your task
To find out why.
♦ He may be uncomfortable from a back injury, a badly fitting saddle, or your poor riding.
♦ He may feel playful or overexcited.

Above: **Bucking that starts suddenly can be due to a back injury or poorly fitting saddle.**

To discourage it.
Check the possible reasons above. If the bucking is just high spirits:
♦ Lunge him before riding.
♦ Ride him forward strongly if you feel a buck coming.
♦ Sit up tall.
♦ Keep your reins short, and tug on one hard.

Above: **Is your pony saying, "Whoopee!" or "Ouch!"?**

it's a fact!
A change of scene, situation, or approach can sometimes miraculously solve a problem. Even ponies with very troublesome habits can sometimes forget to do them when they get to a new yard!

Above: If your pony starts to gain speed, don't just pull *(left)*. Sit tall, and use half-halts to steady him *(right)*.

My pony jogs, rushes, or runs away with me

problem 11

What's going on?
A pony that jogs or rushes could be uncomfortable from bad tack or bad riding. Or he may be just full of more energy than he knows how to handle. When a pony really runs away with his rider, things are serious.

Your task
To persuade your pony to relax and slow down.
♦ Check that all tack fits comfortably. His teeth may need rasping.
♦ He may be getting too much feed.
♦ He may not be getting enough exercise.
♦ Are you sure the rider isn't riling him up or has unsteady hands?
♦ Ponies in too much of a hurry need quiet, relaxing rides with steady companions. Avoid racing or wild canters every time you reach a stretch of grass. Choose circular routes for your rides.
♦ If jumping gets him excited, ask your instructor about schooling exercises that will slow him down.
♦ Control is important, but don't go right to a more severe bit. Sometimes changing to a rubber snaffle or bitless bridle can help. A change of noseband or the addition of a martingale may be enough. Consider a stronger bit for confirmed rushers because it is better to be able to stop with a light touch on a stronger bit than to have to haul back on one the pony takes little notice of. Ask your instructor's advice on a suitable bit and how to fit and use it properly.
♦ Respectfully handle and ride your pony.
♦ Think about your riding, and work on making it more effective.
♦ For a pony that jogs, don't hold him back or be afraid of using your seat and legs positively to drive him on to take longer strides and work up into his bridle.
♦ Take control. Rushers need a rider who can handle the situation. Learn how to use a half-halt to steady your pony any time he even thinks about gathering more speed than you want.
♦ Use give-and-take squeezes on the reins. Don't just pull — the pony will pull back harder. If he gets in control, give sharp tugs on one rein only. If there is space, turn him in a circle and spiral inward, keeping your hands low.

If your pony tends to rush off, avoid overexciting him on rides. Don't always canter in the same place.

Glossary

aids — signals given by a rider to communicate with a horse or pony.

bred — mated with another member of the species in order to reproduce.

canter — a three-beat gait by a horse or pony that is similar to, but slower than, a gallop.

cob — a short-legged, stocky riding horse.

cold-blood — a heavy breed of horse used for work on farms, for transportation, and in industry.

crossbreeding (horses/ponies) — when a horse/pony of one breed is mated with a horse/pony of another.

crosspole — a small jump made using two poles set in an X. One end of each is supported on the jump stander, with the other resting on the ground.

domesticated — the condition of being tamed.

dressage — the execution by a horse or pony of precision movements in response to signals from a rider.

equine — of or relating to horses or the horse family.

farrier — a professional trained to care for and fit shoes on a horse or pony's feet.

flehman — the "laughing" expression a horse or pony makes for the purpose of pushing aroma back toward the Jacobsen's organ.

foal — any young horse or pony up to the age of one year.

gelding — an adult male horse that is not able to breed.

habituation — teaching a horse to overcome nervousness by getting him used to objects he is naturally afraid of.

horse — a large hoofed animal of the Equidae family that is over 14.2 hands high. A hand equals 4 inches (10.2 centimeters).

hot-blood — a horse purebreed of very fine quality, like the Arabian or Thoroughbred.

instinct — a natural, inherited response to stimuli.

Jacobsen's organ — an ultrasensitive part of a horse's body where smells are analyzed.

mare — an adult female horse.

mated — joined together (a male and a female) for the purpose of producing offspring.

napping — a refusal to go forward.

oxer — a type of jump that has width as well as height. It is made of more than one set of jump standers.

pony — a large hoofed animal of the Equidae family that is under 14.2 hands high. A hand equals 4 inches (10.2 cm).

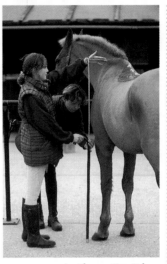

Above: **Don't be overly ambitious. Choose a pony that suits your size and experience.**

Below: **Above all else, have fun with your pony. Then you'll be a long way on the road to avoiding the worst of pony problems.**

predator — a creature that hunts other creatures for food to survive.

prey — a creature that is hunted for food by other creatures (called predators).

spook — describes a motion when a frightened horse or pony quickly moves sideways.

stable vice — an obsessive behavior by a horse or pony, such as crib-biting or stall-walking, that is brought on by boredom or stress. The behavior is a way for the horse or pony to cope with the stress.

stallion — an adult male horse that can breed.

standers — supports that hold up poles or fillers that are used to make showjumps. Standers are usually made of wood or plastic.

warm-blood — a horse breed created by crossing breeds (usually a mix of hot-blood and cold-blood).

withers — the ridge between the shoulder bones of a horse.

For Further Study

Books

50 Careers With Horses. Bonnie Kreitler (Breakthrough)

The Adventure Starts Here. Carol Lynn Pearce (Mayapple Imaging)

Great American Horses (series). Victor Gentle and Janet Perry (Gareth Stevens)

Horse and Pony Care. Tim Hawcroft (Crescent Books)

The Illustrated Guide to Horse Tack. Susan McBane (Storey Books)

Magnificent Horses of the World (series). Dr. Hans-Jorg Schrenk and Tomás Mícek (Gareth Stevens)

The Man Who Listens to Horses. Monty Roberts (Random House)

The Nature of Horses. Stephen Budiansky (The Free Press)

The Saddle Club (series). Bonnie Bryant (Gareth Stevens)

Treasured Horses (series). (Gareth Stevens)

Above: Bond with your horse or pony, and you will have a true friend.

Videos

The Horse Family. (International Film Bureau)

The Horse Whisperer. (Disney)

Horseplay. (Anchor Bay)

Horses Close Up, Very Personal. (Increase/Silver Mine)

Horses and How They Live. (AIMS Media)

Horses and People. (Agency for Instructional Technology)

Horsin' Around: Animal Adventures with Jack Hanna series. (Library Video)

Monty Roberts. (Twentieth Century Fox)

Mythical Horses. (Dorling Kindersley)

Web Sites

www.horse-country.com/

www.horsefun.com/

www.equiresource.com/

www.equus.org/

Some web sites stay current longer than others. For further web sites, use your search engines to locate the following topics: *dressage, history of horses, horses, ponies,* and *Przewalski's horse.*

Index